Above the Crowd

Above the Crowd

Lorna Kalaw-Tirol

Artworks by
NONOY MARCELO

Anvil

Above the Crowd
Lorna Kalaw-Tirol

Copyright © LORNA KALAW-TIROL, 2000

Illustrations © NONOY MARCELO, 2000

All rights reserved.
No part of this book may be reproduced
in any form or by any means
without the written permission
of the copyright owner and the publisher.

Published and exclusively distributed by
ANVIL PUBLISHING, INC.
2/F Team Pacific Bldg.
P. Antonio St., Barrio Ugong
1604 Pasig City, Philippines
Tels.: 671.1899, 671.1308 (sales & marketing)
Fax: 671.9235
Email: pubdept@anvil.com.ph

Cover art and design by NONOY MARCELO
Digital manipulation by ANDY LIZARDO

ISBN 971-27-0852-7

Printed in the Philippines by
OROGEM INT'L PUBLISHING CO., INC.

In memory of my parents,
Jose Manguiat Kalaw and Nelly Mayo Kalaw,
who were, and still are, always there for me.

FOREWORD
A Talent for People

Age-old is the question: what is history? Is it events or people? Some say that Magellan made history with his voyage. Others argue that the voyage itself was history using Magellan merely as a tool to accomplish what it wanted done.

A parallel question: what is news? Is it happenings or people? It is complained that a man who murders his wife is news, whereas a man who keeps his wife for 50 years without murdering her is not news. But here the man-bites-dog rule comes in. The man who does not murder his wife for 50 years is as ordinary as the dog that bites a man; whereas a guy that murders his wife is as revolutionary as a man who bites a dog.

In media the excuse of *"Trabaho lang ito, walang personalan"* does not obtain, for news is always both public and personal. Because the President is such public news, the most privately personal things about him are news as well. And this goes even for celebrities during their 15 minutes of fame. Win in a TV quiz show and you find yourself being interviewed on your grandmother's lovers and whether you sleep in the nude.

Well, maybe that proves that news *is* people. This Age of Information has certainly been removing the fronts from our houses until all that's left between us and the audience on the street is a clear, well-lighted space, like the fourth wall in theater. If this invites the gossip column and blind item, it also inspires one of the blessings and delights of modern journalism: the profile.

The profile has by now been developed into a lively art form that can till any field: from politics to showbiz, from science to religion. It's biography with the starch knocked out. It's news with heart. Or it's info gone impish. Whatever the hat, it now engages the talents of the best reporters: meaning book authors. One American magazine, *Vanity Fair*, is devoted entirely to profiles.

Profile-writing demands wit, style, mundanity, but above all a talent for people: meaning genuine interest in all kinds of characters: good, bad, and what the hell. If you're an interested reader, they'll make interesting reading.

It's my pleasure to say that Lorna Kalaw-Tirol has all the qualities of a good profilist and that my only complaint about her very entertaining profiles is that they are too short. One ends up always asking for more.

One reason is her penchant for giving us unexpected astonishing glimpses of her subjects: the very proper Boots Anson-Roa, for instance, eloping with her Pete and spending with him "one unmarried night which necessitated premarital confession before a priest!"

Or how about this picture of Miriam Defensor as U.P. coed being picked as corps sponsor:

"The first time she was informed of the cadets' choice, she dismissed it as a practical joke. She even turned it down (but) finally gave in to the persistent cadets. At the first meeting of all the sponsors, Miriam gave a short talk. She frankly told the young and pretty girls whom she noticed scrutinizing her that she felt she did not deserve the honor... Miriam received two anonymous letters from coeds telling her 'it was too nauseating reading about you.' But this Ilongga is not one to let such things get her down."

Can you imagine Lino Brocka as a Mormon missionary? And in a leper colony in Hawaii yet.

"The lepers were not allowed to come close to non-lepers. There was always a segregation, even in church. We would stay in one corner, they would stay in the other. They were not even allowed to come into our homes. We built a chapel. I had never worked manually before, never mixed cement, never even hammered a nail before. You know how it is in the Philippines, there's always someone to do those things for you. Anyway, when we finished the chapel, we had a party, but the lepers couldn't join us. I felt very bad."

One of the most surprising quotes is from John Gokongwei back in the days when if you said John Gokongwei, everybody asked: "John *who*?" Said that pre-empire John:

"You've got to think far into the future. You really have to project yourself five years from now. Informally, consciously or unconsciously, you have to ask yourself, where are you going to be? Because if you're not going to be there and you don't have the tools to get there, somebody else is going to be there, and it's just going to be too bad for you."

The entire Gokongwei piece is choice reading, but again is much too brief. It would make terrific exegesis expanded.

Mrs. Tirol and I were together in editorial environs for years when I was younger. So you can guess how horror-stricken I was to learn this book of hers is to celebrate her *golden* birthday. I didn't know that at my back that winged chariot was hurrying so near!

Anyway, this collection of profiles should create a bit of a stir if only because it goes back into an earlier chronology in the lives of people rather altered in circumstance now, like Cory Aquino and daughter Kris. And as evidenced by my samples, the quotes touch and tickle. In reportage, a talent for people means providing them with an encouraging eye and a good ear.

NICK JOAQUIN
National Artist for Literature

Preface

Twenty-eight years ago, I spent a long, exhausting day trying to wangle a few uninterrupted minutes with a tiny teenage singing sensation from Bicol named Nora Aunor. Three months later, Nick Joaquin, my editor at *Asia-Philippines Leader*, sent me on yet another showbiz assignment: to track down 17-year-old Vilma Santos, then filmdom's hottest young star.

By the time I was through squeezing my cassette tape dry trying to turn an uninspired interview into a spirited story, I had sworn to myself I would never touch entertainment people again. It was agonizing to wait for them, and frustrating to coax them to say something of real substance.

But just as every aspiring reporter, male or female, must go through the rigors of the police beat, so too must neophyte magazine writers be baptized with showbiz fire. Then, as now, readers — and advertisers — demanded showbiz stories, and editors naturally wanted to keep their readers — and advertisers — happy.

Thankfully, even though I would be asked to take on more entertainment-celebrity assignments, I had seen the last of the monosyllabic teen idols. Even five-year-old Sheryl Cruz proved to be a much more exciting subject.

The Hilda Koronel who sat down with me for an extended interview was out of her teens and in full bloom — bright, articulate, confident, forthright. The reclusive Lolita Rodriguez was charming and utterly unaffected. Even Kuh Ledesma the "ice queen" was a likable and accommodating subject. Boots Anson-Roa lived up to her cheery Pollyanna image. And Lino Brocka was himself — fantastic raconteur, outspoken social activist, compassionate human being.

Showbiz folk they all were. Definitely "above the crowd." But this book is also about cultural artists, individuals who have enriched Filipino culture with the originality of their vision, the uniqueness of their talents, and the passion of their commitment.

Thirty-one years ago, a tall, slim-waisted girl named Cecile Guidote took me to Fort Santiago and showed me the spot where she wanted to build the first open-air theatre in the country. She was going to call it the Raha Sulayman Theatre. Twenty years ago, Gilda Cordero-Fernando set aside her short stories and became a trailblazing publisher of beautiful books with invaluable help from Cora Alvina and Nik Ricio. Some twenty years ago, too, Alfredo Roces left martial-law Philippines in search of freedom and new challenges to his creativity. Nonoy Marcelo, on the other hand, gave up New York and returned to Manila with an unrealized dream. In the mid-Eighties a teenaged Lisa Macuja electrified audiences in the ballet-crazy USSR. In Manila Susie Winternitz enchanted Filipinos with her magical ways with bamboo and *walis tingting*. Nora Daza was still the undisputed queen of Pinoy cooking on TV, and Petronilo Bn. Daroy was gaining recognition as Manila's most literate dealer of antiques.

Here is how they were before their childhood dreams came true — how Aba Dalena got her start as a visual artist, and how Kris Aquino yearned to become another Sharon Cuneta; or, like Onib Olmedo, Fernando Modesto and Auggie Cordero, how they were before fame changed their lives and their careers; or, like Gang Gomez, before they responded to the call of an altogether different drummer.

Here, too, are the late Luisa Linsangan's secrets of success as *the* women's magazine editor; Bibsy Carballo as talent manager to the stars; stage actress Joy Soler as a wife in limbo.

Nick Joaquin's foreword mentions profiles that do not appear in this book. Let me explain. Nick had written the foreword for a book of 50 profiles titled *Public Faces, Private Lives*. Publisher's instincts dictated twin volumes in place of a thick, unmanageable one: thus, *Public Faces, Private Lives* and *Above the Crowd*.

Since this book has been in the making for close to three years, the update at the end of each profile may not be the latest word on the subject. The past, anyhow, may be more interesting than the present, and remembering it a thoroughly absorbing and rewarding indulgence.

Acknowledgments

In my 32 years as a journalist, I have been blessed with some of the best on-the-job teachers anyone in my profession could wish for, and with colleagues who trusted me enough to give me the breaks I needed. I wish to acknowledge them (in the order in which they appeared in my life) and to thank them for their trust and/or their immeasurable contribution to my professional growth:

Eugenia Duran Apostol, Juan L. Mercado, Oscar M. Rojo, Vergel O. Santos, Rustico E. Otico, Rodolfo T. Reyes, Teodoro M. Locsin, Sr., Gregorio C. Brillantes, Nick Joaquin, Jose F. Lacaba, Tarzie Vittachi, Mark (David) Lewis, Blanche D. Gallardo, Eduardo R. Sanchez, Gilda Cordero-Fernando, Monina A. Mercado, Rosario A. Garcellano, Norma Olizon-Chikiamco, Melinda Quintos-de Jesus, Letty Jimenez-Magsanoc, Domini Torrevillas, Sheila Coronel, Joaquin R. Roces, Amando Doronila, Kunda Dixit, Dick Pascual, Malou Mangahas.

I thank Bibsy M. Carballo, my journalism teacher at St. Theresa's College, for having made my transition to professional journalism so much easier, and Jullie Yap Daza, for having bothered to reply to a college student's request for advice on how to get started as a journalist.

I acknowledge the support and friendship of colleagues and staff at the various newspapers and magazines where I have worked, but especially those at *The Manila Chronicle* (pre- and post-martial law), *Asia-Philippines Leader* (1971), *Philippine Panorama* (1982–pre-1986 snap election) and *Sunday Inquirer Magazine* (1990–1995).

In putting together the profiles for this book, I was fortunate to have had the generous assistance of the following: Rod Reyes and Nik Ricio, who lent me their copies of *Celebrity* and *Goodman* magazines, respectively; Joe Lambino, who allowed me access to the newspaper files of *The Daily Globe*; Ludy Licayan and Cipring Frias of the *Philippine Daily Inquirer* library, who helped me find some of my *Sunday Inquirer Magazine* articles; and the library staff of the Lopez Museum.

I thank Ricky Lo for his valuable updates on some of the subjects of my stories.

On my fourth collaboration with them, I thank once again Anvil Publishing's Karina Bolasco and Ani Habúlan: the first for her enduring faith in my work, and the second for her remarkable patience.

Finally, I wish to acknowledge the unwavering love and support of my family: my husband Vic and our sons Jo-Ed and Paulo, my sisters Josie and Elsie, and my brothers Boy and Val.

Contents

Foreword: A Talent for People by Nick Joaquin, *vii*
Preface, *xi*
Acknowledgments, *xiii*

Ninoy's 'Baby': Very Much Her Own Person, *2*
Getting to Know Nora — And Liking Her, *12*
Lino Brocka, Missionary, *20*
Bibsy Carballo: Taking Things As They Come, *26*
Auggie Cordero: In the Lions' Den, *40*
Gilda, Nik, Cora and A(nother) Book, *46*
Move Over, Niño; Here Comes Sheryl Cruz, *54*
Aba's Menagerie, *62*
Pete's Angels and Other Antiques, *68*
Nora Daza on TV, *74*
On His Way to the Top, I Met Gang Gomez, *80*
Cecile Guidote's Dreams for Theatre, *86*
Hilda Koronel Off The Cuff, *92*
Kuh Ledesma: Singing is My Life, It's Me…, *108*
Luisa Linsangan: The Women's Woman, *116*
Lisa Macuja: On Her Way Up, *122*
Nonoy Straight Out of Marcelo, *134*
Fernando Modesto's Erotica, *146*
Onib Olmedo: Sunshine Boy, *150*
Boots Anson-Roa: Somebody Human, *158*
Alfredo Roces: The Artist as Person, *170*
Lolita Rodriguez: A Real Winner, *182*
If Vilma Comes, Can Edgar Be Far Behind?, *196*
Joy and Pio de Castro: Not Your Usual Love Story, *202*
Susie Winternitz Returns to Nature, *210*

Above the Crowd

Ninoy's 'Baby': Very Much Her Own Person

The spirit of Ninoy Aquino is vibrantly alive in his unpretentious bungalow at 25 Times Street, Quezon City – in the framed photographs of a pensive Ninoy and a laughing Ninoy, in the collage of family pictures taken during the happy years in Boston, in the same pensive pose reproduced on a white lampshade, in the painting of a Ninoy-shirted young woman cradling a child. And this same evening one finds Ninoy's spirit in his youngest daughter, Kristina Bernadette.

As voluble and entertaining as her father, Kris, who was born on the last hour of Valentine's Day 1971, is obsessed not with politics — although she does want her mother Cory to be president — but with showbiz. A year ago, on the top-rated television talk show "Viewpoint," she startled and amused viewers and the program's staid host by announcing that her fondest dream is to star in a movie. Taking the cue, one director did talk to her and her mother and came close to signing up Kris for a film whose story line she herself had suggested. That didn't materialize, however, and Kris tells why in the following account based on an interview with her.

Kris, who first disarmed the public in 1978 as her detained father's youngest campaigner, has shed her baby fat and is now a pretty, creamy-skinned high school sophomore at Colegio de San Agustin. She has co-hosted "Discorama," debuted on the modeling ramp and made the cover of several women's magazines.

A few days before her father's birth anniversary, she shares her memories of him and talks with childlike candor, and at times an amazing maturity and a sensibility that would have done her father proud, of how the assassination and her own painful homecoming changed her life.

Kris Aquino

I still think of my Dad a lot, but not in a grieving way. I just remember little things, like sometimes I glance through a book and I remember. Or when my Mom mentions him. Or I see a sticker. I think I've gotten over the worst. It's true that time heals all wounds.

When I watch the film of the assassination or see pictures of it I feel numb. It's okay, it's what happened. You get to know the truth. It's a choice between living happily with a lie and living not so happily but with the truth. But I'm happy. I thank God that I'm okay, I didn't go crazy or something. He gave me strength. I don't mind talking about the assassination, but you go on from there. You adjust.

I guess I miss my Dad most when I hear other people say things about their own Dad. "My Dad just came home from somewhere and brought me..." Or "My Dad will kill me..." But it's okay. My Mom is always there.

I used to get scared going to the library at home. It was sort of eerie. But it's okay now, I feel that Dad's at peace. I dream about him. Once I dreamed that it was election day and my Mom ran and my Dad came home but he was a baby. He came down from heaven. He said there's a rebirth in heaven. I think he wants to assure us that everything is okay.

I was six or seven when I first asked my Mom why my Dad was in prison. She said Marcos put him there. Then she explained about the charges. I think I even asked, "Why, did he really do it?" She asked me if I believed he was capable of that. I said, "No, I don't think so." She said, "There's your answer." Now I realize how dumb the question was.

To me it was normal not to have my Dad with us; for my cousins and friends it was normal to have their father. I was more concerned then about Sanrio, Hello Kitty, Little Twin Stars, so it wasn't a big deal that he wasn't there. Having Mom here was an advantage; we were always secure.

I was seven when I campaigned for my father. I remember Doy del Castillo came one day and told my Mom it would be a good idea to have me speak. He wrote my speech and made me memorize the names of 21 candidates. They said for a seven-year-old that was something. But I have a good memory, like my Dad. I can remember things, especially conversations. They call me "tape recorder" at home. When I'm waiting for my Mom in her office and people are talking, I hear all of their conversations.

People might say I didn't enjoy giving all those speeches, that I was exploited, but I really did enjoy myself, even if I had to miss school for three weeks afterward because I got sick and I got skin infections. But it was worth it. It was such a blow when they lost.

When we used to visit my Dad in prison I remember thinking that we were like "John en Marsha," you know, about how small their house is. When I was young it was my favorite TV show. At Christmastime we usually slept with my Dad and the room was so small, but it was air-conditioned.

I used to sleep with my Mom. One Christmas my Dad came home and I asked, "Where's he gonna sleep? Isn't his house there?" I had trouble picturing him at home. It was weird, but anyone in my position would have felt the same way. When I was growing up there was only my Mom, so I thought, why is Dad suddenly here?

In the States, it was hard to adjust to having him around, but not to going to school there. I'm aggressive. On the first day of school, when the teacher asked how we spent our vacation, I was the first to raise my hand.

One of the things I remember about my Dad is this TV special on Jacqueline Kennedy, with Jaclyn Smith. Jackie's stepfather won her over with a horse. My Dad said, "Kris, *papayag ka ba,* if I die and Mom remarries, and your stepfather will give you a horse?" No, Dad, I said, and he was shocked and he said, "What did I do to deserve this?" I said, "I want a Snoopy." At that time I really wanted a big, big Snoopy that cost $300. I kept nagging and they said if we go home how are you going to take that with you? I always remember that when I see a Snoopy. Dad was always cracking jokes.

If he were still alive today, I can't imagine him living here, going to school to pick up my report card. That's not possible. When I was on "Viewpoint" exactly a year ago, someone asked if I thought of my Dad as a hero. I said he loved his people enough to come home, not caring about the circumstances. Not many men would have had the guts to do that. He loved people a lot. He loved his country a lot also, but what did this country ever do for him? Mostly pain. If I were in his place I wouldn't have felt the same way. He was generous with others but not particularly with himself. Not like me — I always think of myself first. I guess that's normal. But he always said, we don't have to be that rich, we should think of all those poor people out there.

IN SCHOOL there are a lot of military men's kids because San Agustin is near Fort Bonifacio. So my classmates and friends ask me how I feel about so-and-so. I said it's okay with me, they haven't done anything to me anyway.

Sometimes I hear comments directed at the family like, "*A, basta, KBL pa rin ako.*" It happened once at the airport with some Saudi workers. I'd be plastic if I say they don't bother me. But I tell myself, why should I care about them, maybe they're just insecure or something. Maybe they have problems. It doesn't happen often, not often enough to make a difference. God always has a way of making up for things. If I feel depressed something usually happens to me and everything is better.

When I'm feeling bad I write poems. The poems are therapy; I keep them for myself. I wrote a lot of them in the States. They encourage creativity there; here it's always what's assigned. My Dad always said my main objective in writing poems was to make the words rhyme. Sometimes some of the words don't have connections anymore.

There are times when I wish we were back in the States. I was addicted to soap operas there and I miss them. And I miss snow and having sweaters and I miss steaks so much 'cause I'm a meat eater. I went back there in the summer of '84 with my Mom. No, we didn't go back to our house there. What's the use of going back?

But if I were in the States who'd care who I was? There are so many advantages to being here. For example, I could never have gotten front-row tickets to the Menudo show, never have gotten inside the airport to meet them. And the clothes here are so accessible. It's also fun to be recognized, like when I'm shopping, but it's not normal. Still, I don't think people make that big a deal about the fact that I'm Kris Aquino. Personally, I don't think so. Sometimes it even proves to be a disadvantage. Because people have this notion that you're really goody-goody. That's why my Mom is so careful. She's too good, I don't think I want to be like her. She has all these ideas... she always says you have to be happy with what you have.

To be honest, I want my Mom to be president. She'll kill me for saying this. I pray for that. God, make my Mom president. I'm really the only one in the family who feels that way. There are so many dangers if she runs. And what if she doesn't win? My Mom doesn't want it; I can't force her.

No, I don't have a father figure now. It's just my Mom — she's enough. When I was growing up I was never spanked or belted. My Mom always talks to me. I remember I used to hate going to the dentist. When I was six I didn't want to have some teeth pulled so my Mom didn't let me watch TV until I agreed to go to the dentist.

I've really always been the baby in the family and it's hard to get that notion off. Viel, who comes just before me, is 24. But I don't mind, like if I want to make *lambing*, when I want to get something. Now, though, there is a new baby in the house *(her eldest sister Ballsy and brother-in-law Eldon Cruz's firstborn – LKT)*.

My *Ate* (Ballsy) picked me up at school one day and she was so shocked to see all the boys, how big they were. And she said that if Dad were alive he would never have allowed me to go to that school. My sister Pinky was just telling me that when she went to parties she had to be home by 9:30 p.m. I don't really go out that much anyway, just to a party once a month, and always with my cousins. I usually stay home. Yes, I do find some boys interesting. But that can wait. That's for my Mom's ears. I have to wait till I'm 16 to have a boyfriend. I'll wait, that's okay.

I guess my Dad and I had a lot in common. I got my astigmatism from him. And I read a lot but unfortunately, not what you'd call good reading material — Mills and Boon and Silhouette. But

I've read Iacocca, Danielle Steel, usually bestsellers, what my Mom reads, and local magazines, especially about the movies. Like my Dad, I like to be around people. I won't mind if attention is focused on me, not like my sisters. We both like to perform — he through speeches, me through singing. I've been taking singing lessons from Diane Serrano (female soloist of the brothers-and-sister singing group The Nailclippers) once a week since February. I'm not that good but I'm really trying. I sing modern pop songs — Menudo because it's easy, and Madonna's songs. I used to take tennis and swimming and guitar, but ballet and I quit after a short time.

I REALLY WANT to join the movies. I've been thinking of that since I was three or four when I wanted to be like Niño Muhlach — a child star. I watched all his movies. Then when I was in the States someone sent me a tape of *Dear Heart*, Sharon Cuneta's first movie. I saw it more than 20 times. I said I wanted to do something like it. My Dad used to tease me about that.

Yes, I am really preparing for a movie career the best I can. I believe that if it's something you really want and if you think you can handle it, then go for it. I know what my limitations are; the things I'm not so good at I try harder at them. I haven't been able to do anything about dancing, though, because it's hard. I have no coordination for it. At the fashion show where I modeled there was dancing, so it was difficult. *(As Cory Aquino teases her daughter,* "Parang tatay din niya, hindi sumasayaw. *Talking okay, but dancing is something else." –LKT)*

I see at least two Tagalog movies a month. Of course I watch English movies also on Betamax. That's what my Mom does for recreation on weekends. She's seen only one Tagalog movie since getting back from the U.S. and that was *Kapit sa Patalim*. My sisters hardly ever watch, so I go with the maids or sometimes with my cousins or my school friends. I observe the acting. The last one I saw was *Bakit Manipis ang Ulap*, with Janice de Belen directed by Danny Zialcita. I was thinking it could have been my movie.

Actually, all the plans were ready for a Danny Zialcita movie for me. My Mom approved the script, which came mostly from an idea I had, and we were about to sign the contract. Anyway, I changed my mind because of Menudo. When they were here in April the Del Rosarios of Viva said they would make a TV special of Menudo. I got blinded by the idea of Menudo. I said I'd rather wait for Viva. I guess that wasn't a wise decision because nothing happened. I was embarrassed to face Danny Zialcita when I changed my mind. I remember it was a Wednesday and we were having lunch with them, and for the first time in my life I was quiet.

I've learned from that. Anyway, if that movie of Zialcita's did not push through it was God's will. It wasn't meant for me. If I'd done that, then there would be no more because my Mom will allow me only one. At least now I have something to look forward to. I have to think positive or I'll go nuts.

Every night I pray, Dear God let me make a movie. I'd rather make one than none at all. I hope my Mom changes her mind. Rules are meant to be broken. Once a priest-friend of ours was teasing me that he wanted to appear with me. Mom said, "Kris, promise Father that he will be in one of your movies." Well, she said *movies*.

We talked with Mother Lily (Monteverde of Regal Films) about a month ago. At Regal they don't show you a script first. They want you to sign right away and my Mom wanted a script. That's what makes it so hard. Also, my Mom doesn't want me to have a leading man. That's one of her conditions. And I guess she'll be there every shooting day.

I always think of how I want my movie to be. I want to play someone poor, like a Cinderella story. I'm a good crier, I have an active imagination, I fantasize a lot, I'm a dreamer. When I'm reading a book or watching TV or a movie, I laugh at the funny parts, cry over the sad parts. My sisters say I'm weird.

All my friends think I'm weird for wanting to go into the movies. They say it's *baduy*. I don't think my Dad would have objected. There's nothing wrong with being in the movies. I don't know why people make such a big deal of it. All you're doing is something you like, enjoying yourself, making money for it, in the process when people watch it for a few hours they can forget their troubles. I won't be corrupted or anything like that. I don't think the producers would do that. What would they get out of it?

MAYBE, if I don't enter showbiz, I could write. Maybe I'll take up journalism. I also want to design clothes. I enjoy buying *tela* and having it made. I would love to get into the fashion business. But I also want to have kids and I want to finish school.

I'm in San Agustin now because Poveda (Learning Center) wouldn't let me come out in movies or TV or magazines. But I'm enjoying myself at San Agustin. We do get a lot of homework. I'm not big on studying, but when it comes to exams I really study. In school we get a gold eagle, a red eagle, or a blue eagle, depending on how we do. I got the gold eagle for an average of 90 and no grade below 85. I was so surprised! My Pilipino is okay, but it's my lowest.

I do my homework after doing a hundred push-ups and leg lifts every night. I enjoy eating. I can't diet because then I'll stop growing. And if I don't exercise I'll get fat, and who'll want to get me to make a movie? I used to go to a Greenhills slimming salon, but I gave up on that and decided to exercise at home.

How would I describe myself?

I'm open, I'm normal, I think I'm conscientious. I know what my faults are and I'm not ashamed to say sorry. Sometimes I can be stubborn. When I fight someone I just won't talk to that person for several months. But I'm loving, affectionate. I'm sensitive.

I want to be a successful woman, to be my own person, basically the same as I am now, but more mature, more decisive, and stronger, able to fight back.

Am I interested in politics?

Politics doesn't seem like my thing. But Ronald Reagan started in the movies, so...you never know.

Philippine Panorama
November 24, 1985

Kris Aquino has fulfilled her childhood dream of a showbiz career, starting with guest appearances on television specials in 1987. When she turned 18 in 1990 she made her first film, a comedy with the late funnyman Rene Requiestas. More films followed, many of them forgettable and of the "massacre" genre, although she was nominated for a best actress award for Fatima Buen. Despite her hectic schedule, she managed to graduate from Ateneo de Manila University in 1993 with a bachelor's degree in literature. In 1994 an on-screen partnership with married actor Phillip Salvador, 17 years her senior, led to an off-screen romance that produced a son, Joshua Phillip, born in June 1995, and caused Kris's mother more pain, the former president intimated, than even her husband's assassination. In the last two years, Kris has found her niche as a highly paid television talk show host. Her movie career has been dormant since she became a mother, but in 1998 she agreed to do a film with presidential son Jinggoy Estrada, mayor of San Juan, Metro Manila. In late January 1999, two weeks before turning 28, Kris ended her relationship with Phillip Salvador. In typical showbiz fashion, they both claim that they are still friends. Kris has since been reconciled with her mother, at whose anti-charter change rally on her father's 16th death anniversary she was the enthusiastic emcee.

Getting to Know Nora — And Liking Her

You're no diehard Nora Aunor fan but here you are, at 9:30 Monday morning, waiting, as others would wait for Godot, on the terrace of the star's Better Living home. Except for a fiftyish matron and her teenaged son who have come all the way from Lingayen, and four giggly fans, the house is surprisingly quiet. The maids are tidying up Sunday's mess; the darling of the household is still asleep.

No one in her family dares rouse Nora Aunor from her sleep. For why begrudge her much-needed rest from a schedule taxing enough for someone who is not quite 18? Until two this morning she was taping her show at KBS. The night before, she and Tirso Cruz III were crowned as the Number Two love team of local movies. The coronation, according to two tabloids and a Tagalog daily which every day headline Nora stories, was riotous, with the fans throwing the Rizal stadium into an uproar. The usual reaction to a Superstar.

You yourself marvel at the phenomenon that is Nora Aunor. You've seen her a few times on television. The voice is superb, the manner rather stiff. Her following is fantastic. The maids talk of nothing else; they know her whole life story. But it isn't just the maids. Nora is not purely *bakya* stuff. Not anymore. Your nieces from St. Theresa's and their friends from Maryknoll and Assumption, who before would never be caught dead holding Nora's picture, trooped to *Lollipops and Roses* to see ex-La Sallite Victor Laurel and found Nora okay, too. There's no ignoring the Golden Voice. Jeepney drivers invariably tune in to a radio program that gives breathless accounts of Nora's day. A 10-minute ride can turn you into an authority on Nora Aunor.

NORA AUNOR

No wonder even Imelda the Fabulous could not rest until Nora had set foot on Malacañang. The woman whom the people will install as official lord and mistress of the Palace in '73 must not alienate herself from the people. Nora Aunor could bridge the gap between patroness of the arts and Filipino masses. Is Nora making a movie with Bongbong?

In the charmed circle that closes in on Nora, you're in if you can call her Guy, Tirso Cruz III Pip, Victor Laurel Cocoy, and Guy's chief bodyguard Pae. There are other aides, also female, but they are, you suspect, acting in an unofficial capacity. Together they constitute an almost impregnable cordon sanitaire. Bouncers, someone cracks. Right now, they're fuming mad over a news report that Nora was kidnapped the night before. They've just come from the newspaper office but the reporter was not around. What do these press people want from Guy? they want to know. And they find out you're from the press, too, and they all leer at you. But this is a legitimate magazine, you try to explain, hoping they'll understand what you mean.

Around 11 o'clock you catch a glimpse of Nora at the top of the stairs. She's not about to come down, she only wants to find out what the commotion downstairs is all about. A delivery boy from an air cargo company has arrived with a large box for her. From Victor Laurel, he says as he winks at the fans whose number by now has multiplied. There are squeals of delight, and then speculation as to the contents of the box.

Meanwhile, your patience is running out. So: "Can we take pictures of Nora in her room?" you ask one of her guards. She looks at you with apprehension, then suspicion. After going up and down the stairs thrice, ostensibly to ask her ward's permission, she says yes, but only one shot. So you find the Star herself, in maroon shirt and pants, seated on a circular bed, reading the tabloid article on her supposed kidnapping. She's taking the news better than her friends are. No eye makeup hides the dark circles under her eyes. The face looks tired and drawn. But the person is polite and kind. And she doesn't complain. The breakfast tray is untouched; she's not hungry, she says. Framed photographs of a smiling Pip adorn the dresser and the night tables. He's her only leading man who seems to enjoy that privilege.

Down in the sala, the fans have grown into a horde and they mob her as she makes her way to the car. She's so tiny you can hardly make her out in that crowd.

There are more fans outside KBS and inside Studio 1. Most of them are high-school girls on their lunch break. They wait much longer while their idol winds up her audio taping at the recording room. Here you see the real Nora: self-assured, playful, funny. She makes faces at the technicians in the booth, breaks out in girlish laughter at a joke, clowns with her guests on the show. This is not the Nora Aunor you've seen on TV at all. You find yourself actually liking her. Okay *talaga*.

After six hours of merely watching her, you realize that Nora is at her best when she sings and when she's with her fans. Somebody in the audience calls "Nora, Nora" as she stands in the middle of the set waiting for her cue, and she calls back, *"Hoy!"* She comes onto the stage in a micromini and boots. Someone hollers "Legs!" and she pretends to hide her face in shame, all the while giggling to herself. Onstage she looks fragile and helpless, a little girl wearing size $3\frac{1}{2}$ shoes, until she opens her mouth to sing. Then everyone gapes in awe.

You've been hoping for the last nine hours to have a chance to interview her. It looks like you'll have to wait longer. She hasn't forgotten you, though. Between takes she comes up to you and apologizes. It's all right, you say — and you mean it. After all, this girl hasn't had anything to eat since morning. A real trouper. When the director calls for a break, Pae drags her to the canteen before she can accept any more autograph books and pictures for signing. So you finally get your chance.

YOU'VE BEEN dying to ask her about her pilgrimage to Malacañang. She's very willing to tell you about it. It was on a Monday while she was taping her show that her director, the daughter of KBS boss Roberto Benedicto, told her Imelda wanted to see her. She was excited, of course, but she couldn't imagine what the First Lady could possibly want from her. She was off to the Palace the next day, at 11 in the morning. With her, aside from Pae, were Benedicto himself, his daughter (whom Nora calls

Ate Kitchie), and another KBS executive. There was an added treat in store for her. She met the President and some Cabinet members, of whom the only one she distinctly remembers is Defense Secretary Juan Ponce Enrile. She and Marcos exchanged pleasantries, after which she was ushered into Imelda's receiving room. The First Lady was very nice, a lot nicer to the Superstar than when, as the 13-year-old champion of *"Tawag ng Tanghalan"* years back, she was first invited to Malacañang to sing at Imee's birthday.

This time Imelda was the seasoned politician. How would Nora like to stay in the Palace so she could continue her studies together with the Marcos children? Nora would have a private tutor, the same one perhaps under whom people say the Marcos girls have been studying since the resurgence of violent demonstrations early this year.

Imelda the singer also appeared very much concerned about the young girl's musical career. Nora, she said, should have voice lessons, she can't always be singing in the same style. The First Lady was extremely generous. She offered to send Nora to the States so she could learn from Burt Bacharach and Dionne Warwick.

The First Lady had obviously kept herself up to date. She knew about Nora's 15-day hospitalization and about all the brickbats that fly the young celebrity's way. Don't get involved in any *gulo,* she said as parting advice. And come visit us again.

There was no mention of politics during the two-and-a-half-hour meeting. Yet Nora, although thrilled by the attention given her, is reluctant to accept Mrs. Marcos's kind offers. *"Mahirap nang tanggapin,"* she explains.

What surprised her was the speed with which news of her visit to Malacañang traveled — and to the other party. A hearing of the Tower Productions-Sampaguita Pictures case was scheduled in the afternoon of the same day. On seeing Nora, Sen. Jovito Salonga, her lawyer in the case, remarked, "How did the meeting with Mrs. Marcos go?" He gave her the same advice Imelda did: don't get involved.

Will she or won't she? And will it be Imelda or the Liberals or Cocoy's pa? She gropes for words when asked about the possibility of her supporting Salvador Laurel's bid for the presidency. You notice the La Salle Greenhills ring on a chain around her neck. Cocoy's, no? Yes, she says, blushing, but it's just a friendship ring. They must be very good friends, for she has very special words for the young Laurel. Her other leading men are collectively *mabait* but Cocoy is different: *"masyadong gentleman, maalalahanin, ibang-iba."* He seems to fit her image of The Man: someone who would not be ashamed of her, gentlemanly, kind. You think you detect a glimmer in her eyes when she speaks of Cocoy, but maybe it's your imagination. After all, those were Pip's pictures you saw in her room.

There is much more you want to ask her, but she hasn't taken a bite of her dinner. The fans outside have pressed their faces against the glass doors and windows of the canteen. Nora obliges them by eating with her hands. It isn't a gimmick; this girl is not one to forget her past. She has been accused of gimmickry by sectors of the press so that she no longer knows what to do to please them. Now she does what she thinks best: she is herself all the time. And it's a fascinating self.

Too bad the real Nora is obscured by hangers-on and opportunists. They make you feel sick in the stomach. Nora Aunor is much too nice to deserve their kind.

Asia-Philippines Leader
April 23, 1971

Nora Aunor was back in the spotlight in 1998, 30 years after singing her way to fame and then weathering all kinds of crises—from a failed marriage to rumors of substance abuse to homelessness to a sagging showbiz career—as one of presidential candidate Joseph Estrada's secret weapons (the other being his best friend Fernando Poe Jr.). Movie reporters blame the Superstar's downfall on her unprofessionalism. Two years ago she wanted to revive her moribund singing career, but her unprofessionalism again got in the way. Even a drama series given her by a television station fizzled out after only a few episodes. A respected showbiz writer says Nora is her own problem. But while she may not be the box-office queen she used to be, her acting talent is undiminished. At the Cairo Film Festival two years ago, she was named best actress for her performance in Flor Contemplacion: The Movie. *Her short-lived marriage to actor Christopher de Leon has been annulled. Their son Ian has tried the movies, but has not enjoyed the success his parents have.*

Lino Brocka, Missionary

Lino Brocka is not wearing what he likes to call his Gregory Peck ambience, "the important me" — the Rikki Jimenez-suited, English-speaking, strictly formal, dignified self he puts on when he has to attend cocktails at, say, the American Embassy. He is being his casual self now, in denims and loafers, a little aloof with someone he is meeting for the first time, but gradually warming up as he speaks of a subject dear to his heart, and growing more articulate as the tape recorder on his dining table tries frantically to keep up with him.

Home to Brocka is a modest bungalow in a compound just behind the old KBS building in Quezon City. The living room looks somewhat familiar, parts of it anyway: the wicker sala set with batik cushions that the director explains are souvenirs from Chanda Romero's pad in the film *Inay*. Two or three cabinets in the living and dining rooms belong to Laurice Guillen, who recently moved into a condominium. Brocka himself doesn't have very much, aside from his TV set and his stereo and his roomful of books, nor does he care to own much. "I don't like to have too many things to take care of," he says. "They tie you down, and I'm the sort who likes to just be able to disappear, go somewhere, when I feel like it."

These days, though, he is busier than he has ever been in his 10-year directorial career. He is making one movie after another and, to his critics' assertion that he has gone commercial (*Hayop sa Hayop*, widely advertised as the Hilda Koronel boldie, is a Brocka quickie that took only 17 days to shoot), he shoots back, "I have never made a film that I am ashamed of." He does admit that he has to work nonstop because he has debts to pay off. CineManila, the film company he heads, has gone bankrupt, he explains, and he is taking full responsibility. "The money I earn (*Brocka gets*

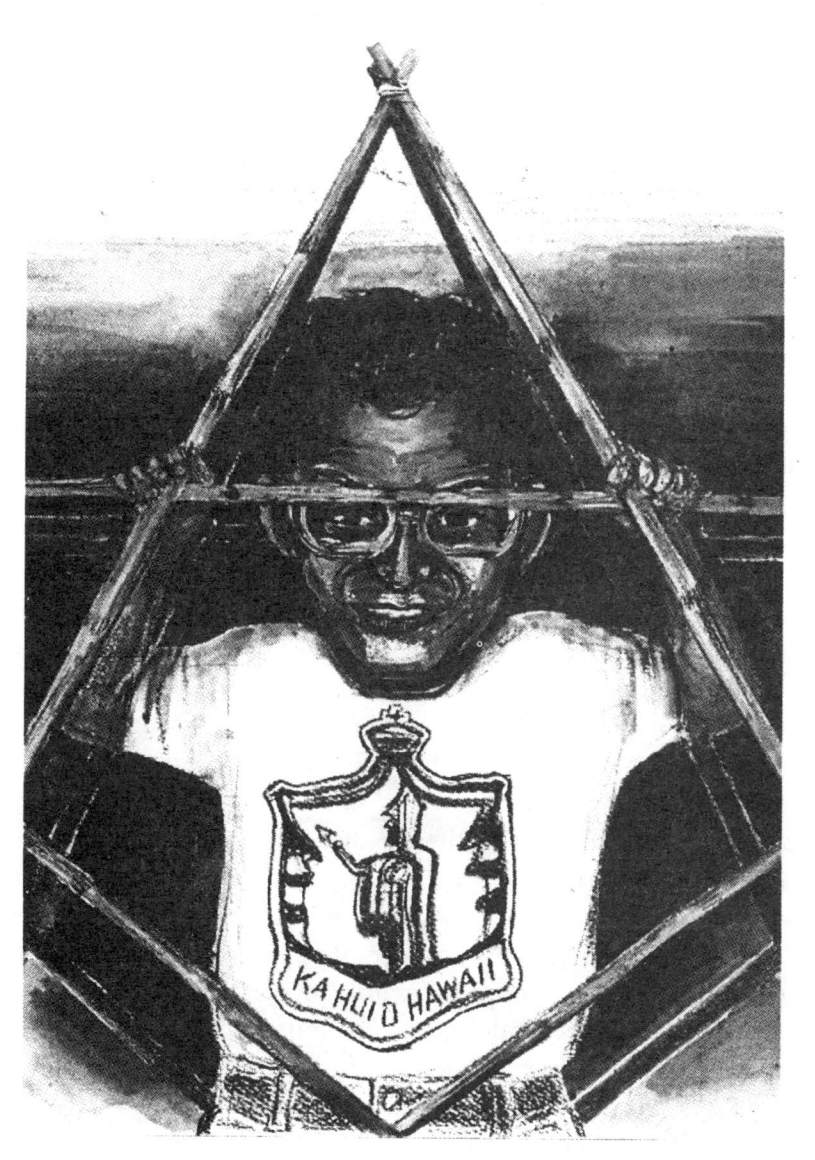

LINO BROCKA

P80,000 per movie – LKT) goes to the bank." By next year, however, when he will have settled all his obligations, he would like to go back to doing only two movies a year and giving more of himself to the young people of PETA.

Theater has always been his great love, even at the University of the Philippines where he was an overstaying student (few U.P. overstays can beat his 10-year record) enrolled in the English literature and later, the Speech and Drama course. He never graduated. "I liked to study, but I couldn't stand math, chemistry, zoology, anything that had to do with figures. But I had 196 units in English, more than was required. For an M.A. I flunked U.S. history four times. And I couldn't stand ROTC. Behn Cervantes, who is a friend of mine, got an exemption from ROTC. His doctor said something about a trembling of the extremities. Well, he had connections, I didn't."

When Brocka was 21, he fell away from the Catholic Church and became a Mormon, one of the first Filipinos to be converted. "It wasn't the fault of the Catholic Church, but the fault of my own orientation. I needed help, but I wasn't able to separate the personalities from... I was so priest-oriented." Four years after his conversion, he was sent to Hawaii as a missionary and from there, to Molokai. The leper colony was known as The Rock among the Mormon missionaries, and how Brocka got there is a story in itself.

A missionary is sent there either to punish him or to shut him up. I was sent there because I was voicing out some opinions against the system. I didn't like the way things were being run, so I had to speak up. Since I was a convert, I was more questioning, analytical, objective about the whole setup.

"Molokai, of course, meant lepers. So there was an apprehension *na baka mahawa ka,* dread at the mere mention of the name. The first time I got there, I was all alone, and the people who were supposed to meet me didn't come. I felt like crying. I was so lonely. I asked myself, why am I here?"

But Brocka came to love the island and its people.

"It's a beautiful place, the most beautiful spot in Hawaii. It has what are called the topside and the downside. The topside is where the other communities are, and there is a steep, steep cliff and a narrow strip down to the other side. The strip was the trail made by the horses which were used to take the food down to the lepers. No one below 18 is allowed in the colony and anyone who goes down must first be fumigated. When I was there, the population was 280. The patients were a mixed group — there were Chinese, Japanese, Americans. All of them were deformed, of course. The first time I saw them I couldn't look at them. And there was the stench of *nana*. But they didn't feel ill at ease; they even joked about their appearance. They had terrific spirit, really positive attitudes. They were always laughing and joking. They were the funniest people I'd ever met.

"The lepers were not allowed to come close to non-lepers. There was always a segregation, even in church. We would stay in one corner, they would stay in the other. And there were holes in the church for them because they were always spitting. They were not even allowed to come into our homes. So I would talk to them while they stayed outside the gate. I remember when we built a chapel. I had never worked manually before, never mixed cement, never even hammered a nail before. You know how it is in the Philippines, there's always someone to do those things for you. Anyway, when the chapel was finished, we had a party, but the lepers couldn't join us. I felt very bad."

In the 18 months Brocka spent on the island he staged speech and drama festivals, taught the people the dances of his country, ran errands, evangelized. And he grew up. "When I was in the Philippines, I was drowning, really. But Molokai changed a lot of my attitudes. When I came back, I knew I had grown up. I was no longer young when I went there — but those were my growing up years. It was a beautiful experience."

Brocka spent two Christmases in Molokai, the first at the topside, the second at the downside. "I was with another missionary, an American. Our cottage was right beside our church on a hillside, about a mile away from the nearest neighbor. One day I told my companion that back home we made star lanterns at Christmas. I had never made a *parol* in all my life, but we went to town anyway and bought some Japanese paper and found some bamboo. Our star was very crudely done, but it was a star and we put a bulb inside. We were coming home one day and we could see our star from afar. My companion stopped the car, got off and said, 'Brocka, look at our star. You have beautiful Christmases if this is the way you celebrate them back home.' He said it was like Bethlehem, seeing that star a mile away from home. He couldn't get over it. He would stop the car every night just to look at our star."

Brocka's downside Christmas was not so happy. "That was when I really missed home. Everybody was opening presents, there was a lot of partying, but I didn't feel part of it."

When Brocka left Molokai the lepers had a going-away gift for him. It was a beautiful handmade Hawaiian quilt they themselves had worked on, painstakingly, with the stumps that their arms and hands had become. When some tourists later offered to buy the quilt from him, for quilt-making in Hawaii is a dying art, Brocka politely refused. Today it is one of his prized possessions.

The Molokaians saw Brocka off with a serenade of his favorite Hawaiian songs. All he could do was cry. "I couldn't even kiss them when I left."

And so, in memory of his friends in Molokai, Lino Brocka had, as one of the major characters in his deeply moving film, *Tinimbang Ka Nguni't Kulang,* a leper. And from his days in San Francisco, USA, where he spent three of his post-Molokai years, during which he subsisted for a month on tacos and candy and water, and competed with the hobos at Golden Gate Park who scrounged in garbage cans for the leftovers of weekend picnickers, and learned to balance five glasses on the palm of one hand as a busboy in Alioto's, and listened to tales of loneliness in a home for the aged, Brocka shored up many more insights for future use. It is no accident that his films are so rich in understanding of, and compassion for, the human condition. That is why we can forgive Brocka his quickies. For more often than not, what he gives us is a cinematic gem.

Celebrity
December 31, 1977

Lino Brocka made films that stirred the public conscience and during the dictatorship angered First Lady Imelda Marcos for their raw portrayal of social realities. His movies were shown in the Cannes and Berlin film festivals and helped draw world attention to Filipino cinema and talent. A fighter all his life, Lino was a vocal opponent of film censorship and a political activist during the martial-law years, especially after the assassination of Ninoy Aquino. When Cory Aquino became president, she appointed him delegate to the Constitutional Commission, but he resigned the position after becoming increasingly disillusioned with Mrs. Aquino's positions on sensitive issues. In 1991 he was killed in a car accident. He did not live to see himself honored in 1996 as National Artist for film and broadcast art, in recognition of the new consciousness in Philippine cinema that his movies created.

BIBSY CARBALLO
Taking Things As They Come

Ma. Dolores "Bibsy" Carballo reigns supreme in a tiny dominion called *Butingting*. The name, which connotes a dabbling in everything and anything, is really rather apt. Once upon a time, when leather tooling was in vogue, *Butingting* referred to a store within Bibsy's PR office that sold personalized leather items. Business was good; nearby, after all, were the faddish *colegialás* of St. Paul College and the students of the University of the Philippines College of Medicine. The store earned enough to pay for the rent. Now that leather ID bracelets are passé, the *Butingting* sign points to a *sari-sari* store just outside the office where boxes of Breeze stand beside cans of Dutch cleanser on a shelf and Sunflower biscuits vie for attention with Marlboro cigarettes. A little sign tacked to the wall says the store also sells homemade palillos and cinnamon rolls, and accepts typing jobs besides. A calendar pinup of Gina Alajar, wrapped in electric blue feathers, keeps the salesgirl happy company.

As in times past, this store does well enough to help cover the rent. So that when scandalized friends like *Panorama* editor Letty Jimenez Magsanoc exclaim, "*Naku naman, Bibsy*, why do you have a *sari-sari* store? *Nakakahiya naman!*" she is quick to retort, "*Bakit, anong nakakahiya diyan?*"

Her office isn't much to look at either, if you're looking for a public relations outfit that oozes pizzazz. The paint on the wall — it must have been pristine white when Bibsy moved in 12 years ago — is dirty white and peeling off. The batik tapestry draped over a tall shelf is faded. The desks and chairs are functional and mismatched. One surmises the driftwood chair is there to complement the seashell and coral arrangement atop a steel cabinet. Atop an olive-drab cabinet are volumes of Blair and Robertson's

Bibsy Carballo

The Philippine Islands, some of them still partially wrapped in brown paper. A volume of *The Best of Life* lies beside discarded photography equipment on a high shelf. A touch of pop art is provided by a Del Monte tomato juice waste can in red and green. And looking bewildered in the midst of all this earthly business is a three-foot-tall *santo*.

The office derives its character mainly from the pictures that cover the walls: photographs by prizewinning lensman and cinematographer Romeo Vitug, mounted advertisements of films Bibsy has promoted, several small H. R. Ocampos, an Edwin Diamante surrealist painting, two portraits of Bibsy by Alfredo Roces and Tiny Nuyda, a Stevesantos rendering of an air mail envelope addressed to Gerry Delilkhan.

Into this tiny office, cooled only by a couple of electric fans, strides Bibsy Carballo on a late afternoon. A late riser, she does not come in until after 12, but today she has been out talking business with Lino Brocka. She heads straight for her desk, looking anxious, and starts reviewing the list of the day's phone callers. She scrimps on everything, even paper, says a former employee; the scratch pad on which the daily list of callers is scribbled carries news briefs from the National Press Club. The phone list adheres strictly to a formula: name of caller, time he or she called, purpose of each call, the person's phone number. Any item overlooked by her two secretaries can ignite the Carballo temper, which, however, cools down just as fast as it flares up. Satisfied with the day's list, she sits down to make her own calls. First, she makes an appointment with a recording executive to discuss a song an old American friend of hers has written. Then she makes a long distance call to Baguio to report to another friend on the progress of a film project they are collaborating on, hopefully for the Manila International Filmfest next year. Between calls she talks about a couple of coups: Christopher de Leon has agreed to do a walk-on part in *Bangag*, the play she and her Ma-Yi associates are staging in August; and a young man wants to talk to her about managing his talented wife's career in entertainment. A final call is made to a magazine editor about a possible pictorial of Anthony Castelo's innovative *barongs* and perhaps later, another pictorial for another of her clients, the Champoy duo of Noel Trinidad and Subas Herrero.

It is after five and Bibsy has not had lunch. She's a very hard worker, says her old friend Margot Baterina of *Panorama*. "*Kahit gutom na gutom*, she will work until the job is finished." Margot was among Bibsy's friends who were shocked and dismayed by her decision to go into movie PR from journalism. The field is *bakya*, they told her. "*Gaga ka ba*," Margot recalls Bibsy replying, "that's where the money is." Her timing could not have been more perfect. The declaration of martial law had caught her writing documentaries on a freelance basis for Channel 5, so that whether she had stayed at the *Manila Times* or opted for television, she would still have been jobless come September 21, 1972. Then old friends started asking her to handle the promotions end of their projects: Conchita Sunico for the Manila Symphony Orchestra, the Laurels for a concert Cocoy was staging and the film career he wanted to launch, Lino Brocka for his comeback film, *Tinimbang Ka Nguni't Kulang*. Lino had been her classmate at the University of the Philippines. Until he got her interested in movie PR, the only Filipino film she had seen was Tessie Agana's *Roberta*. When more film accounts came her way, she found herself rushing to see movie reruns and revivals. Before she knew it, she had enough clients to keep an office going. There were, among the earliest ones, the CCP Dance Company, Repertory Philippines, musicals, concerts, Bancom's *Ang Kiri*, some of them short-term, others exclusively hers. And then, of course, the movies.

"Bibsy is very much her own woman," says another old friend of hers, *Mr. & Ms.* publisher and editor Eugenia D. Apostol. "She had to go on her own."

"When I started in the movies," Bibsy recalls, "Lino said, 'Don't say this is fantastic, the best ever. Just say what we're trying to do.' *Tama naman*. You invite critics, other people, to review a play, you let them give their opinions. My policy is just to bring something to their attention. If they see value in it — and there usually is — *hindi na mahirap*. But if the Manunuri write an unfavorable critique; *wala ka nang magagawa*."

She has always been a positive thinker who has no need for

Science of Mind, and an incurable optimist ("a cockeyed optimist," says Letty Magsanoc) — "I don't believe that there is a totally negative person. There is something good in this person, in this product. You'll always find merit in something, in some a little less than in others. So I have a product, which I think is good. My responsibility is to bring it to the attention of media — look at it, *kung hindi mo* type, *di hindi, siguro* type *ng* somebody else."

With her optimism and positive thinking, she claims there has never been any product she had great difficulty pushing: "Some are more marketable than others, *pero wala iyong walang tumatanggap.*" Her list of accounts, in the recent past and at present, as far as she can remember, includes Leonor Goquingco's Dances of the Emerald Isles, the Philippine Educational Theater Association (PETA), Filipino Heritage, Casalinda, Aawitan Kita Productions, Rex Humbard, Octoarts, the Ballet Federation of the Philippines, Pitoy Moreno, Ben Farrales, Joanne Drew, Sensei and Dansei grooming salons, *Flor de Luna*, even All-Star Basketball. In the movie industry, she has promoted films for Agrix, Lea, Bancom, Regal, Lotus, Cine Manila, Four Seasons, Premiere, Sampaguita, Trigon, Sining Silangan, Ian Films, NV Productions, Communication Foundation for Asia (CFA) Movie Masters, Pera Films. She manages, besides Anthony Castelo and Champoy, Kuh Ledesma, Boots Anson Roa, and most recently, Isabel Rivas.

Her positive attitude extends to her dealings with potential and actual clients as well. "I always look," she says, "at the experience of meeting a new person in a positive way. *Meron tayong pag-uusapan;* you can give me something *na hindi ko alam.* I haven't met anyone yet *na wala akong nakuhang bago.*" Perhaps, she muses, her openness to learn from anybody and everybody explains why she gravitated toward the PR profession. "They say in this profession you have to be plastic." She shakes her head: "I've never felt pressured to do that. *Layasan ko siya pag naiinis ako.*"

Basically, her PR philosophy is to accent the positive. With the individuals she manages, she makes it a point to discuss and come to an agreement with them about the points to be emphasized. "There are certain things they don't want said, although if some people stumbled on something about my client, *wala na akong magagawa.* First of all, the natural personality has to come out. I don't think you can totally manufacture something. Like Kuh. Okay, she's aloof, *suplada*. Turn that into an advantage. She hasn't changed. We don't tell her to be nice because people see through that niceness. *Kawawa* ang client if she is made to play a role. Now let's take Boots. I cannot tell her to be a little bit controversial only because people think her being too nice is boring. The one and only time she blew her top was when she walked out of her morning TV show. I suppose you could say we took advantage of that; we made sure everybody knew about it. I felt that writing about her walkout would answer all the criticism *na hindi totoong tao si Boots dahil hindi marunong magalit.*"

Although she believes every product, event and person is marketable, she has rejected some accounts. "*Hindi ko kaya,*" she explains. "I feel I really cannot contribute. I tell them frankly that I don't know what to do." An apolitical person, she says she wouldn't accept political clients. None, however, have come her way.

There had been criticism in the past that her style of promoting was purely "A" and that her clients were heavy on the cultural side. "For a while *lahat daw ng hinahandle kong sine hindi kumikita.*" (These included films by Brocka, Ishmael Bernal and Celso Ad. Castillo.) She does not dispute the elitist label pinned on her, admitting that most of the films she promoted did poorly at the box office, but now that she has started handling Regal movies also, she feels that she no longer deserves the typecasting. Besides, she adds, she also did the promotion for the blockbuster *Sierra Madre*. She is quick to clarify, however, that the Fernando Poe-Ramon Revilla casting coup was an example of a film that hardly needed promoting precisely because of its terrific cast.

While learning the ropes of the PR profession, Bibsy admits that it helped to have friends in the media. That, however, was not enough. "That was only one-third of the work done because you could be feeding them the wrong thing and your PR would have the opposite effect." Her style is to supply press people with a steady stream of press releases and audiovisual material, with a journalist's keen perception of what each particular publication would have use for.

"You build up a relationship with the press," she says. "All I let them know is what *si ganito, si ganoon* are doing. They tell me if they're interested or not. I try to sell the idea of a feature on a person and the publication assigns a writer to do it. I usually don't write about my clients, but sometimes I do." There are people in the media she likes more than others "but there isn't anyone I hate. I think if you know how to deal with them, if your approach is open, they will also be like that."

Her old friend Letty Magsanoc has an "aversion for PRs" but "Bibsy is different: she pushes very hard but does so subtly. The style is soft-sell but not exactly." Like, if Bibsy wants to push a girl for the *Panorama* cover, says Letty, she will arrive at the magazine office with complete audiovisual equipment on the client and without saying a word, will proceed to interest her friend in her proposal.

"Bibsy is no run-of-the-mill PR, but a thinking PR," says Thelma Sioson-San Juan, the *Times Journal*'s Living Section editor. "She knows what editors will buy or not buy." Thelma particularly credits Bibsy with finding an appropriate angle for the people or the projects she's promoting instead of sticking to the standard style of press releases.

Evening Post movie editor Ronald Constantino cites Bibsy for being "honest without being offensive." He would even venture to say that with her professionalism and competence, she is the best PR around. "She's very adaptable, mixes very well with people," says Constantino. "With her you don't have to measure your words or be on your guard. She is very fair with people, whether on a professional or personal basis."

Even with the Filipino movie press, Bibsy rates highly. Says Baby K. Jimenez, PR girl for Christopher de Leon and Nora Aunor, "Bibsy is very effective, very professional." She ranks Bibsy among the three best movie PROs in a field where she estimates there are 10 or 15 legitimate practitioners.

"There's a lot you can learn from the Filipino movies press," Bibsy says. "They have a lot of initiative, a sense of competition which you don't see in the dailies." She suffers, however, in comparison with those of her colleagues who make it a point to attend every birthday party in filmdom. "As far as my work is concerned," she says, "*tapos na* by 6 p.m. As a rule, I don't go to their parties and that counts a lot most of the time. *Pero merong iba* who don't care for that as long as you deliver."

Not that she doesn't have friends among movie personalities. Nora Aunor is, she says, a friend, as are directors Celso Ad. Castillo, Romy Suzara and, of course, Brocka. "In the movies it's very hard to make friendships. You're very close for the duration of a project but after that, *wala na*. Maybe you build up a sort of defense; you don't like to come too close because you know that after this, *wala na*. But I don't think movie people are less capable of deep relationships. In fact, they have many characteristics you don't find in others; they're more candid, very open, stronger. They've got guts and the ability to take success as well as failure."

Being also a columnist (she writes a weekly column on the movies for *Parade* magazine and an occasional one on television for the *Times Journal*), she sometimes has to settle a conflict between what she writes and what she promotes. The question had bothered her years before she went into promotions, when as a writer for the *Sunday Times Magazine* she asked Alfredo "Ding" Roces how he reconciled his being a columnist with his running a PR outfit at the same time. She had asked him then whether his clients expected him to praise them in his column. No, Roces had replied, adding that he followed his conscience: if it didn't bother him, then there was no question of any conflict.

She remembered the lesson from Roces years later, when she had to handle Nora Aunor's *Minsa'y Isang Gamugamo*. Lupita Concio, who had been her classmate in graduate courses on theater at the Ateneo, had recommended her to the superstar. "I didn't know how to go about that movie," she recalls. "It was my first time with real movie stars. With Lino and the Laurels, who were friends, I didn't have any barriers to overcome. So I had a contract, in which one item specified that the promotion of the movie would have nothing whatsoever to do with what I write on my own. *Alanganin ako na baka mag-*impose *si Nora*. After that, I made no such specification anymore. I just played it by ear. Other clients did not make such demands. I found out that if you're working with certain people on a project, your being a columnist works to your advantage so you get the scoops earlier. I've had a lot of news that I got first. Maybe if I didn't have a column, I'd feed the news to others. That's the only time I use it to my advantage."

The only "boastful" statement she will allow herself, if it can be called that, is that while she may not get too many movie projects, she does get the good ones — "all the movies which years from now will be considered milestones in Philippine movie history like *Jaguar* and *Tinimbang*." People have the impression, she says, that she is loaded with movie accounts. Not true, she stresses. The most recent one was *Confess*; upcoming films are Regal's *Que Sera Sera*, a musical to be directed by Joey Gosiengfiao, and MVP Pictures' *Batch '81* under Mike de Leon's direction.

Bibsy considers herself lucky that she has had no unfortunate experiences with clients so far. Feuds, yes, such as the "misunderstanding" she had recently with producer Armida Siguion-Reyna over the filming of Bancon Audiovision's *Salome*. She would rather forget the incident, however, and like a good PR person, looks forward instead to the opening day of the film which she is sure will be one of the year's more important movies. The "misunderstanding" with Armida is something "time will heal *kasi wala namang pinag-awayan na grabe*." Charge it to experience, she sighs, and to the fact that she looks on her work as a process of learning. "It's really like going to school. You don't stagnate, you're not just doing one thing. After you get exposed to something new and unfamiliar, *ang ganda*." So that while the money is good (although business, she says, was better two years ago), the self-fulfillment is even better.

How does she measure her effectiveness?

"It's very hard," she says. "I'm always asked, how do I know if I have helped. There's no real way. Like I'm promoting a movie or play. The results are measured by the box office. The movie could have been carried by the cast. With individual clients, on the other hand, my job is just a matter of making their image more total, *hindi kalat na kalat*. Let's face it: even if no one was promoting Kuh, she would still be noticed because she's good. Maybe you just hasten the process."

Speaking on a more personal level, she says, "I think I'm effective because once I accept something I know that I am going to enjoy it. That means you really have to be 150 per cent involved in that particular project, whether it's low-budget or big. Also, the client knows that I mean business. I have this idea that, wow, I'd like to go to the province for two months, and I can do it, too. Somehow that idea is imparted to the client — *na kung ayaw ninyo, iiwanan ko kayo.*"

THE STANDARD QUESTION asked of Bibsy, when people find out she is an only child, is "Are you spoiled?" Her standard answer used to be an adamant "No," until a friend of hers pointed out that it was not a matter of whether or not she thought herself to be spoiled, the fact was she did not have siblings to compete with.

Her father, Captain Ruben Carballo, had been with the corps of engineers in Bataan at the start of World War II. He was killed by the Japanese and his body was never recovered. Months later, when his family was informed of the tragedy, they were also told that he had faced death with great dignity. Bibsy never really knew her father.

She grew up in San Juan town where the Marquezes, her mother's family, and the Carballos occupied two streets. She was never lacking in extended families. She would cross the street, for example, and an uncle's house — and 10 cousins — would be there. She still lives in San Juan today and would not dream of living anywhere else: "I like its small-town ambience; I don't like the artificial villages."

School was St. John's Academy, which was founded and is still run by her maternal aunts. "What bothered me most as a child," she says today, "was having to go to a school run by relatives. If I had a choice, I would have wanted to go somewhere where nobody knew me." Because she was the principal's niece, people said she was the teacher's pet, especially when she finished high school as valedictorian. She went on to U.P. for Liberal Arts with a major in English literature. At U.P. she was Josefina D. Constantino's favorite student ("I really liked her; she gave me an A"); J.D.'s was the only class where she did not play hooky. Despite her lack of seriousness with her studies, Bibsy completed a five-year course in four years by cross-enrolling at U.P. Padre Faura's night school.

"I wanted," she says, "the experience of going from Diliman to Faura by public transportation. I would get home at 10:30 in the evening. *Pero maganda.* I was able to compare the students at Diliman with those at Faura. *Ang mga nasa* Faura working students, *sa* Diliman they were in school because they had to and they didn't appreciate it."

In the middle of her collegiate years she struck up a friendship with Letty Jimenez of St. Theresa's College, who was already then writing feature articles for the teen page of *The Manila Times*, which was edited by Eggie Apostol. Letty, whose father was in the military, belonged to a group of army brats at Camp Crame, and Bibsy the UP coed fell in easily with the gang of La Sallites, Ateneans and *colegialas* whose hangups she could not comprehend but whose parties she enjoyed.

When she finished college, she also joined the *Times*' teen page. It was then that she decided she wanted to be a journalist, so she went on leave from the *Times* to enroll in the graduate course in journalism at Northwestern University in Illinois. She was gone for three years, savoring the independence that comes with being alone and away from home.

When she returned to the *Times*, cartoonist Nonoy Marcelo was astonished. He had never met her before but she struck him as the "*kauna-unahang* women's libber, very gutsy and aggressive: *anong gusto niya, ginagawa.*"

Marcelo christened her "*kagaw,*" which is an old Tagalog term for flea, "*kasi* hippie *siya, hindi normal magdamit.*" In fact she went to way-out designer Dante Ramirez for her clothes, to Bambang at times with Marcelo and the rest of the gang (*Times* feature writers Linda Villamor, Betsy Romualdez and Sylvia Mayuga) for relief clothes. For all her unconventional fashion sense, however, Marcelo swears that on one of Bibsy's birthdays she threw a formal (read: long gown for the ladies) party at her home, with dinner by candlelight to boot.

"I would call myself unconventional in certain aspects," Bibsy explains. "I just like to do what I like to do. I've always been like that. But there are things I don't go for, like drugs. I can't be forced to do something I don't like to do." She cites, for example, the day *Times* executive Isabel Roces sent a comb over to her desk with the admonition that she tidy up her hair. Miss Roces is gone but, Bibsy laughs, "If she saw me now she would send me 10 combs."

When Conchita Sunico offered her a hotel public relations manager's job years ago, she declined primarily because the position would require her to be conventionally dressed all the time. It is well known, for example, that Bibsy Carballo always wears sandals, never shoes, even to formal occasions. Until recently, she wore pants all the time and now that she seems to have discarded jeans in favor of dresses, people are wondering why. Her eclectic fashion sense, as she prefers to call it, was eye-catching enough to put her in a fashion magazine's list of nominees for Manila's best-dressed women two years ago.

Her unconventionality extends to a dislike for nice cars. Although she has a three-year-old Gemini, she still prefers her 14-year-old Beetle, which has neither air-conditioning nor stereo. Superstition keeps her from releasing, but not accepting, money on a Monday, even *if* that happens to be payday. But she is also a highly organized woman who personally stores office files and keeps track of everything in *Butingting*.

Once upon a time Bibsy was a professor — in a *colegio*, at that. She takes pride in the fact that many of the girls who were enrolled in the journalism and, later, communication arts program at St. Theresa's College are now doing well in media, advertising and public relations. Thelma San Juan speaks for all of Bibsy's students when she says, "As a teacher, Bibsy was very valuable to me. Her journalism was not theory. She brought us out to the field, allowed us to mingle with professional newspapermen so that when I joined the *Journal*, I felt right at home. She gave us access to everything in the newspaper business."

Bibsy gave her girls as much leeway as she could. Attendance in her classes was never compulsory; neither was the wearing of the uniform. Her girls were her friends; many of them still are.

"Most of my friends," she says, "are either in theater, or are artists, or are inclined to art. You don't have to read, you just have to talk to someone and you get new insights. That's what I enjoy. I like going home after a good conversation with someone who has brought up a new idea. It's an example of what I consider successes. *Wala akong malaking ambisyon.* The day-to-day little things to me are successes."

Her "little things" are not so little. As one of four women comprising Ma-Yi Associates, she is constantly promoting the careers of new and promising artists or thinking of new plays to stage. *Bangag,* a Tagalog adaptation of a Broadway play on drug abuse and the addicts' rehabilitation, goes onstage in August with Gina Alajar, Jay Ilagan, Johnny Delgado, Edgar Mortiz and Mark Gil in the lead roles. Years ago, she put up Indigo Gallery with artist-friend Bencab. In the '70s she was part of a group that organized the Center for the Advancement of Young Artists (CAYA). The projects fizzled out only because of financial difficulties, never for lack of enthusiasm.

"Frustration *ko siguro,* that's why I get involved in the marketing of these activities," she says. As a child, she had taken piano and ballet lessons; as a teenager, she had a tutor in oil painting. Not too long ago, she even took voice lessons "to clear my sinuses."

She would like to go into sports more seriously, like bowling, swimming, tennis. And to travel, "because getting out of the country at least once a year opens up new things." Her last trip out took her to Cannes with Nora Aunor, Lino Brocka and Phillip Salvador and a side trip to New York on the way home. She is not one to make plans, however, or to map out her life. "I take things as they come," she says, "but once I get into something, then it becomes a commitment."

The idea of marriage, of total commitment, has never appealed to her — up to this point. She needs to know that if she wants to take off, she will and she can. Perhaps later, she laughs, "when I would have mellowed enough to let me do what I want to do."

Right now, she enjoys what she's doing, but feels sure that any day she can leave it. "I know something better will come along."

Celebrity
July 31, 1981

Bibsy Carballo is still an entertainment publicist, handling established movie stars, directors and singers as well as showbiz newcomers. But with the current slump in the industry brought about by the economic crisis, she has gone back to journalism, her first profession. She writes a weekly opinion column in the Philippine Journal.

Auggie Cordero
In the Lions' Den

Auggie Cordero's world at six in the evening of Friday, the 23rd of March, was Room 841 of the Philippine Plaza. In less than three hours he would issue his fashion statement of the year, via the clothes and accessories that now filled every available space in the room. Four racks were heavy with sailor-inspired dresses, leopard-print pants, evening frocks in taffeta. Strewn on one of the beds were ostrich and turkey boas in tangerine, beige, mocha, chocolate, hot pink and white. At the foot of the other bed was a box full of raffia hats; another white box contained flowers. Colored plastic hangers lay atop the dresser; under it were stacked shoe boxes labeled Shoemart.

A barefoot woman quietly pressed high-fashion clothes beside the dresser. Sammy Tiongson, Cordero's assistant designer, wearily examined every single item in the racks. Three of Cordero's favorite models were early birds. Menchu Menchaca, newly emerged from the shower, was drying her hair frantically. Lui Gancayco Gaskell traipsed around the room in an eyelet shirt and long, shapely limbs. Wanda Louwallien was pinning up her brown hair.

The designer himself was not looking good; he never does before a show. He had lost 13 pounds in two weeks and was now running a temperature and nursing a nasty cough. In denim pants and a white T-shirt, he looked pale and famished. The other day, he said, he had lunch at 10 in the evening. All for the love of fashion.

Fashion designers approach this moment in their lives with the same sense of mission and high purpose, perhaps even the same messianic complex, with which Bob Barker announces the name of the new Miss Universe. The Moment for Auggie Cordero, since he hit the big time less than a decade ago, has always been

AUGGIE CORDERO

exciting and triumphant. He has, to be sure, more critics than he deserves, precisely because he is successful. "Filipinos don't like winners" is the way he explains all the brickbats that fly his way from colleagues in his very bitchy profession. "They like underdogs. They'd like to be able to say, *'Oy, kawawa naman si Auggie.'* They can't take it when they have to look up to you. They feel intimidated. You get to be very unpopular if you're successful. If you land in a foreign magazine, they say it's because you have connections. It all boils down to one thing — envy."

And so when he says that he is actually exposing himself to the lions with this show, he is not kidding, even though he's laughing. This year, his 13th in couture, he has come up with a collection that he truly loves. "There is nothing in the collection which I would change, whether it be the color or the accessories. Even if half of Manila or the entire city were to dislike my clothes, I would still feel an inner satisfaction. If I'm too advanced or too much for them, I can't do anything about that."

But the entire city was turning out for this show, or so it seemed. Already, 150 more tickets than the actual 1,200-seat capacity of the Plaza ballroom had been sold and people kept phoning in for more. Someone said Mayor Nemesio Yabut wanted to see the show but could get no more tickets. Cordero was ecstatic to report that Carmen Guerrero-Nakpil, who in 1968 had written that the fashion model "is both symptom and cause of our social ills," and whose daughter Gemma Cruz is now an occasional model in Paris, was coming to view his collection.

"I was so flattered," Cordero bubbled. "The news brightened up my day." The next moment he was on the phone accepting advance congratulations from someone who said she didn't care about the dinner, she just wanted to see the show. Best of all, a newspaperwoman who declared war on Cordero a couple of years ago, when he failed to come up with a dress she needed immediately, was now, the designer said, asking to be invited.

"I know I have a winner," he said, beaming. That winner cost him not only 13 pounds but also P100,000 worth of fabrics and accessories, handpicked in New York and Hong Kong, Rustan's and Divisoria. (At Rustan's alone, he said, his textile purchases ran to P30,000.) Production expenses for the show, which were shouldered by his sponsors, totalled P150,000. And yet, he complained, "people around here don't take fashion seriously." He talked of his "frustrating moments" as a designer, "like when I introduced pants under long gowns and they could not imagine anybody wearing that. Now everybody's wearing it. Sometimes when you're too advanced they find it awkward if they haven't seen it in a magazine. It's a pity — they're hampering the designer's creativity.

There are other "frustrating" moments. Like when he has to spend a whole day just looking for the right shade of lining for a certain material. Or when he wants a particular shade of red but everything he finds is off-tone. Or when he has raffia hats made locally and they turn out to have more flop than flair.

When those times hit him, he wishes he were back in New York, where everything a designer could possibly wish for is readily available. And where there are no good or bad designers because every one of them has a clientele. And another thing: "People here are so conscious of class, status, which shouldn't be the case. You can wear old clothes and yet look very elegant. All it takes is flair and individuality."

Last December in New York, depressed by his first encounter with American winter, Cordero indulged in a real luxury — a pair of handsewn military boots by Giorgio Armani, Milan's top shoe designer for men. The boots, Cordero said, are what he will wear to the show, to complement an all-black outfit. The Moment is all that counts.

But tomorrow, Cordero, who must be one of the truly literate designers around, will go back to the bestsellers on his shelf.

"I have to catch up on my reading," he said.

Celebrity
April 30, 1979

Auggie Cordero is one of the country's most talented and respected fashion designers. He is credited with many trends and innovations, and the few fashion shows he has deigned to mount have invariably won rave reviews from even the harshest critics. He was Cory Aquino's favorite designer when she was president.

Gilda, Nik, Cora & A(nother) Book

"Hanapin mo 'yung bulok na blue gate at bulok na bahay," said Gilda Cordero-Fernando by way of explaining how to find her house. And with typical self-deprecation, which I associate only with people who are sufficiently secure but not smug about themselves, she added, *"Siguro bulok na rin ang mga tao sa loob."*

I found the place, all right, and walked past the *"bulok na* blue gate," through an unpaved driveway, to get to a lovely Japanese-style bungalow that Leandro Locsin designed long before he conceptualized the Cultural Center of the Philippines. And I found the mistress of the house, looking slim and smashing, as she always does, in a short frizz and a black kimono with batik prints. She dislikes dwelling on compliments, this woman who long ago gave me a very definite idea of the kind of woman I would like to grow into in my middle age, preferring to refer to herself as *"laos"* when someone asks, with genuine concern, why she doesn't write anymore. "You must realize when you are already *laos,"* she says with a straight face, "so you must think of something else."

Her "something else," which she thought of four years ago, is book publishing. Her GCF Books first came out with *Culinary Culture of the Philippines,* followed a year later by *Streets of Manila.* Comes now *Turn of the Century,* a magnificent recreation of life and art in the Philippines during the period 1890-1910. Gilda's books are coffee-table books, which means they're horribly expensive *(Turn of the Century* costs P250), but they are selling, not like the proverbial hotcakes, but well enough to make their publisher line up book projects until 1985.

Two weeks after *Turn of the Century* came off the press, Gilda is meeting separately with two sets of staff for two GCF books in the making. The first is *Jeepney,* the text of which Eric Torres of Ateneo has just completed, with photographs by *Expressweek's* Ed

GILDA CORDERO-FERNANDO

Santiago. *Jeepney,* says Gilda, will be smaller than her three previous books and will naturally be, not cheap, but easier on the pocket. The second project for this year is a Philippine version of *Whole Earth Catalogue* and will record, for example, the games and ghosts of our childhood, the superstitions that rule our lives and all the other quaint minutiae that make us so interesting as a people.

Other books in the GCF lineup will tackle small-town Philippines, household antiques, Philippine architecture, family names, and the sociological and psychological sides to being Filipino. "She is a fountain of ideas," says Cora Alvina of her friend Gilda. *"Parang* waterfall."

The "waterfall" is playing gracious hostess this afternoon, presiding over *merienda* of *puto* and *dinuguan* laid out on a glass-topped table in the dining area, where reign a grandfather clock and several antique clocks, none of which tells the correct time. Talk veers towards *Turn of the Century* because Nik Ricio, who designed that book, and Cora Alvina, who coordinated its production, are here. And because I want to find out what goes into the making of a beautiful book.

"Nag-aaway kami ni Gilda diyan," Nik had told me when I saw him in his apartment the week before. *"Dahil sa* deadline. *Tatawagan niya ako sa telepono. Itatanong niya kung ano ang* estimate *ko kung kailan matatapos ang libro. Gagawa ako ng* estimate *pero kung minsan hindi rin nasusunod dahil sa* press. *Mafu*-frustrate *siya. Hindi siya nagagalit, pero alam kong* frustrated *siya. Mamaya, naibaba na pala niya ang telepono, hindi ko alam.* Hello, hello, hello, hello *ako nang* hello, *wala na pala siya.*

"Pag nag-uusap kami ni Gilda ng masamang tono, hindi ko ginagawa ang iba kong trabaho. Pero hindi ko naman alam kung saan ako pupunta. Kalutkot lang ako nang kalutkot dito pero walang nagagawa. O kaya, tulog lang nang tulog."

"Nag-away din sila ni Cora," Nik is saying now, *"tungkol sa* follow-up *sa* press. *Pero noong nagkita sila dito, nag-akapan pa sila, may iyakan pa."*

"Nik and I never quarreled," Cora Alvina clarifies. "We understood each other."

"No, there were no quarrels, really," corrects Gilda. "Frustrated *lang ako. Kukuha ako ng orders, mangangako ako ng date of issue. Tapos, hindi pa alam ni Nik kung ano ang Philippine art nouveau. Nandoon pa rin kami sa Grade One. Maloloka ako."*

She earned a fair number of sobriquets from her staff. Nik and Cora alternately referred to her as Mrs. Panic, Peter Panic, Gobernadora, Madame. And Johnny Reyes, production manager at Vera-Reyes Press who still sounds like the swashbuckling LVN movie star he once was, used to call her *"matanda"*. Gilda herself says that when Nik and Cora felt particularly upset, Johnny would invite them into his office and gently say, *"Huwag na kayong magalit sa matanda. Baka hindi tayo dalhan ng meryenda."*

"We loved Johnny," Cora gushes. *"Pag nagkainisan na,* he would take aside *kung sino ang pinakagalit,* start talking to him or her, crack jokes, and by the time that person left Johnny's office, cool *na siya, nakalimutan na ang galit."*

"Ikuwento mo ang opisina natin," Gilda prods her.

You mean Junque (her Filipiniana shop in Mabini)? I ask.

"Oh, no," says Cora, "it was this coffee shop (which, for reasons that will be obvious later, will have to remain anonymous) in a Roxas Boulevard hotel. It's the lousiest, most inefficient coffee shop in town. They take three hours — one hour before they get your order, one hour before your order comes, one hour before they bill you. We chanced upon the place and decided it was ideal. *Biro mo,* air-conditioned, *okey na okey ang pagkain, walang nakikialam sa amin.* We would all come in carrying a portfolio each, dump all sorts of paper and pictures on the table, flash some slides, exchange material, and nobody minded. It became our office. We would come in at two or three in the afternoon and stay for hours."

When they were not meeting, Gilda would spend hours at the National Library or the Lopez Museum searching for old pictures and books and samples of Philippine art nouveau. Or she would look up nonagenarians whose minds were still lucid enough to recall how life was at the turn of the century. Nik, on the other hand, would sit at his desk on the second floor of his three-story apartment and pore over the art nouveau studies Gilda had provided and photographs Cora had taken of the *gumamela,* the *rosal,* the *sampaguita,* the *ilang-ilang.*

They were the most difficult, the most exasperating part of the work, Nik says of the lavish borders that appear on every page of *Turn of the Century*. Each chapter of the book is set off by a border that suggests its contents; in some of the chapters every page has its own distinguishing border. How to produce art nouveau that was Philippine — that was the problem. Nik would come up with something and Gilda would disapprove it, saying it was Western, not Philippine. He would try again and Gilda would shake her head, again, this time because it was Nik Ricio.

Gilda, in the meantime, had grown attached to Ikoy, Nik's curly-haired baby, whom she would borrow and take on shopping trips to Harrison Plaza while his father labored over the essence of Philippine art nouveau. Nik refused to give up, not just because he had a contract to honor, but because he had his artistic pride to reckon with.

"One thing about Nik," Gilda says, "is his pride. He doesn't give up. *Kahit hindi siya matulog ng tatlong gabi.* I wait and wait and wait and wait until he calls and tells me he has it."

Even now, three books and four years later, Gilda still confesses to being astonished by Nik's talent. "When he gets the essence of an article, he gets it by osmosis. What he did with one of the chapters in *Turn of the Century*, 'Brown Man's Burden,' is a masterpiece of a layout. I simply told him it's the part of the book that really makes a statement. I didn't know what to do with the pictures, how to do the chapter. He did."

No intellectual, and no avid reader either, Nik says he did not even read "Brown Man's Burden." He simply looked at the pictures, among them a shot of a mustachioed American on whose right shoulder sits a monkey, and decided a monkey would do best as a border. We were, if you will remember your history, *tsonggo* to the Yankees for some time.

Nik Ricio says he hasn't even gone over *Turn of the Century* since he got his copy from an ecstatic Gilda. "*Sawang-sawa na ako,*" he says, feigning weariness. "*Biro mo, isang taon kong ginawa.*" He claims he will not do another such book again, even if he's paid four times more for it. He declines to say how much he got for *Turn of the Century,* or even how much Vera-Reyes is giving him for Alejandro Roces's *Fiesta,* to be released late this year. Suffice it to say that Nik Ricio is today's hottest book designer and artist.

Yet books were farthest from his mind when he quit the fine arts course at the University of the Philippines to get a job because all his friends had turned professional. He tried advertising, as an assistant visualizer, and lasted five months. He decided he wanted to go home to Santiago, Isabela, where an uncle of his was the mayor. His Honor kept him busy designing a park for the town and then sculpting the figure of a woman holding stalks of *palay* for the plaza. Nik went into the work with gusto, and he remembers feeling like Michelangelo as people gathered around the statue and watched, awed by the sight of the diminutive young man who could do such a huge job. The statue still stands in the Santiago plaza, but Nik refuses to look at it when he goes home these days. Not even to show it off to his wife Tez.

Nik met Gilda Fernando in 1975 when he was art director for General Motors' *Goodman* magazine and she was on the lookout for an artist for GCF Books. She asked him if he could do the layout for a book; he was interested but didn't know how much to charge her. Of his first job for GCF, *Culinary Culture of the Philippines,* Nik says, "*Naiilang pa ako sa kanya noon. Parang hindi ko alam kung anong gusto niya. Pero ngayon professional na. Pinakikinggan niya ako, pinakikinggan ko siya. Noon ang role ko taga-layout lang.*"

He knows where he stands now, of course. Tez Ricio laughs as she says, "*Gigil na gigil si Gilda sa kanya. Ang asawa mo, sabi niya, hindi ko maiwan.*"

Happily for us who are grateful for beautiful Philippine-made books, even if we can't afford them, the Fernando-Ricio tandem will be with us for a long, long time. Criticism hardly bothers Gilda. Oh, yes, she has her critics who accuse her of elitism and irrelevance. She says, "Even I cannot afford to give my books to my friends. Don't you think I feel bad? But I'm so happy that the books are there. Hopefully, people are getting interested in our books so we're creating a market. *Kahit na ano ang ilabas mo, bibilhin.* But they have to be packaged in an interesting manner." That's the sharp businesswoman in her speaking.

Nik Ricio is taking it all in. He is grinning widely. *"Gusto ko yatang matutong sumulat,"* he says. And Gilda and Cora chorus, "In that case, we'll learn to draw."

All's well with their world. Thank God.

Celebrity
January 31, 1979

Gilda Cordero-Fernando, proud to be 68 in 1998, has set aside book publishing in favor of painting and spiritual pursuits. She has been studying anthroposophy and soul dancing and encouraging others to do the same. In 1997 she helped found the Center for Health and Creative Arts. She delights in organizing people into discussion groups and helping them to find themselves, from women in their sixties and seventies to women who hate their mothers, and in conducting workshops for septuagenarians and older folk. She has illustrated two children's books and co-authored A Spiritual Pillow Book *with Mariel Francisco. Always eager to test her limits, she ventured into fashion production two years ago with a fashion-theater piece and a companion book called* Jamming on an Old Saya. *Always a trendsetter, she will celebrate her 70th birthday four months early (February 2000) by staging* Luna, an Aswang Romance, *a musical on the creatures of the Filipino mythical underworld.*

Cora Alvina, after working on more books and writing a column on Philippine historical vignettes, joined the Metropolitan Museum of Manila and became its president in 1998. Under her leadership, the Met has become a dynamic, creative force in the cultural scene.

Nik Ricio is acknowledged as one of the best book designers in town. He has found time to paint again in recent years, and in October 1999 mounted an exhibition of his oils in New York City.

Move Over, Niño;
Here Comes Sheryl Cruz

She doesn't jump from her seat to greet me with the regulatory (among movie people) buss on the cheek for "*Tita* So-and-So." I am yet another strange face who has come, her mother explains, to interview her for yet another magazine. "No, no, no more interviews," she protests, as she slumps in her seat and covers her face. "*Ayoko na.*"

I like the kind of welcome she gives me. Really. I am relieved to see that Philippine movies' newest child star, Sheryl Rose Ana Maria Sonora Cruz, is being allowed to be herself — a six-year-old child — and not one more zombie animated to smile and be extra nice to every journalist who wants to write about her.

On this rainy afternoon she is sitting with her mother Rosemarie, her brother Wowie and actor Subas Herrero in an unlighted mini-theater at the LVN compound. We are able to see one another only through the light that streams into the doorway. And yet I can see that despite her mother's cheerful company, Sheryl is looking very tired. She has, after all, been here since early this morning to dub her lines for *Candy*, the film her parents have produced to launch her to stardom.

Sheryl is a pretty child who can look sweet and lovable one moment, petulant and menacing the next. The eyes are, as she singsongs in that charming Johnson's baby shampoo commercial, her father's; her lips and nose, her mother's. She is wary of the stranger who has come, not to interview her, but to hear her *kuwento*. It is my tape recorder that does the trick. Upon seeing it, she wants to try it out but is still suspicious. I ask Wowie, who has just completed grade one at the Ateneo, to sing, and fellow Atenean Subas Herrero suggests he do the Blue Eagle Song. Which he

SHERYL CRUZ

does, most solemnly. Forthwith, Sheryl announces it is her turn. She sings four lines from the Hagibis hit *"Katawan."* Then she stops, a little embarrassed at having to admit, *"Iyan lang ang alam ko."* But, she informs me with a bright smile, "I sang that in *Leon at ang Kuting,"* which means if I see the movie I can hear the rest of her song. It is the picture she is making now with real-life uncle Fernando Poe, Jr.

I can see that I am getting somewhere. *"Ang sine ko ngayon,"* she says, *"ay Candy.* Candy is me. I'm *pilya* there. My father is bad. His name is Bernardo but shooting *lang* only. *Ngayon, nagdadabing kami dito."* I ask her, in all candor, what dubbing means. She looks at me, I think mockingly, amazed that someone as old as I could be so ignorant. "Dubbing," she says now with great authority, *"iyong titingnan mo ang bunganga mo, tapos magsasalita ka. Sasabayan mo."* She goes back to the subject of *Candy.* "*Kinidnap ako ng totoo kong tatay. Dalawa ang tatay ko doon. Dinala ako sa bahay niya. Kasi gusto niya akong kidnapin. Iyon lang."*

The man who plays her real Papa in *Candy* is, she says, Jesse Cruz, Ricky Belmonte to you, but to her, "the best, best Papa in the world." Her superlatives do not end there, however. *"Pero ang best na best na Papa si Papa* God. *At si Mama* Mary." She looks *at* me earnestly. *"Dapat ilagay mo iyon. Kasi bibigyan namin ng komiks si Papa God at magpapadala kami doon ng* balloon."

It is so far the only sign she has given that she has been initiated into the SOP of public relations in the movie world, this earnest request to mention God and the Blessed Virgin in my story. I promise her I will.

Why, I ask her, do you like to be in the movies? Her answer— or answers, to be more accurate — come easily. "Because my Papa said. Because I want to be an actress. Because I want, I'm a girl."

Yes, she says, smiling, she likes to watch movies. Hers and her father's, but only when he says it's all right. She also likes to watch television: *"Iyong kina* Mama Inday *ko* (Susan Roces, her mother's sister), *iyong Susana Daldal* (an old Susan Roces picture). *Gusto ko din siyang batiin. Binabati ko din si* Mama Inday *ko at si* Uncle Ronnie. I like *Sesame Street* also and *Muppet Show* and *Ron-Ron the Flower*

Angel and *Candy Candy*, and *Wonder Woman*. I have a costume of Wonder Woman."

She has been talking breathlessly, not at all bothered by the loss of her two front teeth on the last day of shooting of *Candy*. Suddenly, she leans back in her chair, fixes her gaze at me and declares, *"Pero tired na ako mag-talk."*

And, wearing a yellow parka to keep her warm, she runs off and joins Wowie in a game outside the building.

Her mother, who has been sitting nearby all this time, lets go. Rosemarie is no stage mother, not yet anyway. Of her daughter's early start, she says, "Sheryl likes acting, and that's the important thing. You tell her, *hindi ka na mag-aartista, iiyak iyan.* We did not force her to join the movies."

Neither was Rosemarie, who was introduced in a Sampaguita tearjerker, *Ulilang Anghel,* when she was seven. She made the decision herself, after promising her mother she would continue her studies while working in films. "I was taught to make my own decisions early in life," she says, "and I am raising my children the same way." She cites as an example the Johnson's commercial she and Sheryl did when the child was only four. "I asked Sheryl if she wanted to appear on television. I told her it would be hard work. She said yes to me and to the agency people. She couldn't say we forced her. My children understand that when you say yes, you really mean yes."

Rosemarie's approach to motherhood is not one of playing things by ear. Guided by a book called *How to Train Your Child — the Subconscious Mind,* she began training all three of her children from the time they were still fetuses. "I immersed myself in art — painting, the movies. Maybe that's why my children have turned out the way they have. I try my best."

"I want my children," she says, "to be very responsible." If Sheryl, her middle child and only daughter, wants to make more movies, she has her parents' blessings, but only if she can cope with the industry's demands. Eldest child Wowie is not in films because, Rosemarie explains, he is a boy and must take his studies seriously. Wowie, a strikingly handsome eight-year-old, has been told time and again that his role is that of a man: to take care of his mother, his sister, the house and the business later on. "He's very proud of his sister," his mother says when asked if Wowie resents Sheryl's new stature. "I always tell them to love each other and to share."

Between Rosemarie and Ricky, it is the latter, his wife claims, who is the real disciplinarian. "My husband wants the children to be perfect; you know how fathers are." Wowie and Sheryl are spanked for serious offenses; in Sheryl's case these could stem from her possessiveness with her things to her moodiness. "She is," her mother says of the young star's temperament, *"sumpungin."*

"And very *pilya*," her father is to add when he emerges from the dubbing room much later. He recalls the day he and Rosemarie were summoned to St. Paul College in Pasig where Sheryl is in kindergarten, because their daughter had brought some lipstick to class and painted all her classmates' lips.

But Ricky Belmonte is understandably proud of his daughter's varied talents. Sheryl not only acts, she also sings and dances. *"Kahapon,"* her father says, "we had a recording with Ronnie Poe. One take *lang si* Sheryl. *Isang araw ko lang tinuro ang tatlong kanta sa kaniya, kabisado na niya."* "Cruz y*ata,"* Rosemarie says, positively beaming.

Belmonte, star of many an adults-only film, says he will give his daughter all the encouragement and support she needs should she choose the acting profession, but he will never allow her to appear in *bomba* films. His wife laughs. *"Ako nga,"* she says, glancing mischievously at Belmonte, *"nagpapaalam, e ayaw."* The children are allowed to see their father's movies, but only if these are rated "for general patronage." Occasionally, Sheryl and Wowie catch one of their father's old films on television. When they see that he is about to kiss his leading lady, who happens not to be their mother, they turn off the set. For while they understand that their father is a movie actor and their mother a movie actress and whatever they do on the screen is not for real, they probably feel, in their young minds, that what they don't know — and won't see — won't hurt them.

"If you want to see Sheryl cry," her father says, "tell her *ang Mama niya magbo*-bold. *Pero gusto niya sina* Alma (Moreno) *at* Vilma

Santos, one of Sheryl's godmothers)." But that is because, his wife sensibly points out, "Sheryl knows them as persons."

"Actually," Rosemarie says," you cannot say that our life is normal. My life was not normal when I was small. All the time what was normal for me was the movies."

I HAD WANTED to see Sheryl in her home, where I thought she would be in her normal surroundings. I was only partly right.

Sheryl Cruz is just as much at home in Valle Verde, Pasig, as at the LVN compound or on a movie set. Her world is the movies — it has become normal for her to attend school in the morning and shoot a movie in the afternoon. Her parents did ask for the St. Paul nuns' approval of Sheryl's "career." The nuns gave the matter no second thought. "The principal," Rosemarie says, "said nobody can stop Sheryl when it comes to acting." At St. Paul, which is well known for the artistic talents it has nurtured, Sheryl has been in every stage presentation, either as the star or as a minor character. In last year's Christmas program, she was the Christmas bride, the focal point of the play.

These days, reports Ricky Belmonte, "I go to St. Paul and the children say, *'Iyon ang tatay ni Sheryl'*." He is not complaining.

Joey Gosiengfiao, director of *Candy*, says the child has natural rhythm. "It's easy to work with her because she's a girl, she's easy to direct. The most unusual thing about her is she takes directions so easily."

In the tiny room into which we have now squeezed ourselves to watch the trailer of *Candy*, the little star sits up front quietly waiting for the film. When it finally comes, she sees herself being billed as the Child Star of the Eighties, after Tessie Agana of the Fifties, Snooky of the Sixties, and Niño Muhlach of the Seventies. She is unperturbed through it all, even as she sees herself on the screen sobbing, cheering, singing, dancing, laughing. It is only in the final scene, where she is dressed as Wonder Woman, that she exclaims. *"Ako iyon, si* Wonder Woman!"

It is not, after all, the first time she has seen herself on film. She was in *Good Morning, Sunshine* not too long ago, and it was the success of that movie — and the public's warm reaction to her

— that inspired her parents to produce *Candy*. "*Magandang* follow-up," is how Ricky Belmonte puts it.

He and his wife are not, however, about to rob their daughter of her childhood. She is, in many respects, still a little girl who dreams of herself as Snow White, Cinderella, Sleeping Beauty and Wonder Woman (*"Wala akong napapanaginip na mumo kasi binabantayan ako ni* Papa God"); likes to draw (Rosemarie says Sheryl has a very good sense of color); enjoys ballet lessons; has occasional fights with her big brother; invents stories for her parents' consumption; likes nice clothes and dolls and her mother's high heels.

But she is also a little girl who relishes acting all by herself in front of a mirror and cries each time she sees someone on television in tears. Her mother asks, "Sheryl, *sinong nagtuturo sa iyong umarte?*" She points at the sky and says, *"Si* Papa God. But sometimes I listen in my heart."

It does not sound like a rehearsed line.

And as I leave her, lying on her stomach in the dubbing room as she intently watches her *Lola* Chichay go through her scenes, and after she has asked me, in a whisper, what shade of lipstick I'm wearing (*"Ang akin pula,"* she volunteers), I hope in my heart that she will be allowed to be herself. Always.

Please, Papa God.

Philippine Panorama
April 6, 1978

Sheryl Cruz graduated to teenage roles that required her to sing and emote in the movies and on television, and then to so-called bold dramatic roles for film. Even in her personal life, maturity came early to her: some years back her mother abruptly left the country and moved to the U.S. eventually remarrying. Ricky Belmonte is no longer active in the movies, preferring to be a musician. Sheryl's brother Wowie is a struggling B-movie actor who goes by the screen name Renzo Cruz. In August 1996 Sheryl gave up the movies to marry John Norman Bustos, a Filipino-American with the San Francisco police force.

Aba's Menagerie

"Grown-ups never understand anything by themselves, and it is tiresome for children to be always and forever explaining things to them."

-From *The Little Prince*,
Antoine de Saint-Exupery

She made me feel very much like one of Saint-Exupery's grown-ups, this tiny six-year-old child who prattled endlessly as she guided me from table to shelf to table to shelf at Sining Kamalig, where her exhibition of clay sculptures was to open that afternoon.

There, lovingly arranged on tables and shelves, were the fantastic products of two years of a child's sculpturing: ducks and elephants, and kangaroos, snakes and worms, butterflies and shrimp and fish, alligators and owls, lions and tigers and camels and giraffes, a beribboned snail, a horse and a man hugging each other, Kermit the frog and Big Bird, donkey and horses and cows and sheep, Charlie Chaplin with his hat and cane, a witch and a snowman, birds and bugs and frogs, a fierce-looking dragon and some nudes. Occupying center stage on a tall shelf was an orange polka-dotted teddy bear, obviously very much hugged. In front of it was an inch-high teddy, done in clay, one of the artist's very first works.

And there was the little artist, Sabana Lluch-Dalena, denim-jeaned and yellow-shirted, smiling often despite two missing front teeth. She was greatly thrilled about her show, and eager, as a child always is, for strangers to see what she had done. There were 300 pieces in her exhibition, leaving one breathless after viewing them all, but also gasping, how could a little girl have done all that?

But Sabana, Aba to everyone who knows her, is no ordinary little girl. The second of three daughters of highly talented parents

ABA LLUCH-DALENA

(Danilo Dalena the artist and former editorial cartoonist and Julie Lluch the sculptress and ceramicist), Aba has been handling clay and drawing since she was four. She has her mother's open, earnest face and, by her own analysis, both her parents' enormous gifts *("Nagmana lang ako sa Daddy at Mommy ko")*. There has been no pressure on either her or elder sister Isa to show some precocity; as Julie Dalena put it, "This is all hers; there was no coaching, no editing whatsoever." But there has been plenty of encouragement and freedom to explore.

"Iniisip ko lang kung ano ang gagawin ko," Aba said when asked where she got ideas for her sculptures. Not even from books? I pressed. *"Hindi sa book, hindi ko ginagaya."* In fact, she added petulantly, *"Ang Mommy ko, kinopya lang niya ako."* That wasn't quite true, of course, for Aba's nudes are take-offs from Julie's originals, and her fire-breathing dragon is, according to her mother, an imitation of something she had seen her father do.

Still, it is cause for marvel that Aba has been to the zoo only once in her life, but her animals are executed with painstaking detail. Also, a lot of imagination. Her frog, she explained sadly, was shivering *"dahil nabasa ng ulan."* And her cow had round spots on its belly because, well, cows are like that.

Was she selling her animals? I asked. Oh, yes, she replied excitedly, the whole lot would cost P300. But there were pieces she wanted to keep: a sheep for her Mommy, whose favorite it was; a carabao for the family's housemaid; the teddy bear for herself. There were more than three items marked NFS (Not For Sale) at the show's opening. Danny Dalena wanted to keep Charlie Chaplin for himself, for one thing. Plus the Ugly Duckling and one of the dogs.

It was a well-attended opening. There were Aba's *Tito* Nick (Joaquin), *Tito* Pepe (Lacaba) with his wife Marra (Lanot) and son Kris, *Tito* Recah (Trinidad) who incurred Aba's ire sometime ago when he sat on one of her snakes and broke its neck, *Tito* Roger (Ordoñez) and *Tito* Nonoy (Colayco), all of them colleagues of her father from the days of the *Philippines Free Press* and the *Asia-Philippines Leader*. And her mother's friends from the Ceramics Guild, Chinkie Arellano-Ramos and Baidy Mendoza. And more from the literati: Rosalinda Orosa, Hilario Francia, Jose Carreon and Benjamin Bautista. None of Aba's classmates were present but her little cousins were, all of them oblivious to all the praise being thrown Aba's way.

The honoree, still wearing her denims but with purple orchids now pinned to her red and blue shirt, was herself too busy to listen. She was sitting at a table in the middle of the room, a mound of artist's clay and a canful of water in front of her, and a couple of sticks of bubble gum. She would take some clay from the mound, pinch it this way and that, prick it with a toothpick and presto, she had a new animal to add to her menagerie. It was her way of demonstrating to her audience of young and old the intricacies of her art. Yet she was clearly enjoying herself, and not even the ribbing that her father got from his friends *("Hoy, Danny, mas magaling kaysa sa iyo si Aba"* and *"Danny, magkano ba si Aba?"* and *"Mas mabili pa ang gawa ni Aba"*) could faze her. When Toni Serrano Parsons, two young children in tow, asked her innocently what kind of bird she was holding, Aba answered, without looking up from her clay, *"Basta, ibon lang."*

Nick Joaquin was telling friends about the other facet of Aba's talent. She has, he said, a knack for picking out the distinctive characteristic of a person's face when she draws a portrait and while the outcome may not be an exact, detailed likeness, anyone who sees it can immediately identify the subject. Julie Dalena was sorry she didn't exhibit Aba's drawings as well. Perhaps another show, I said. Aba is fast growing up, Julie said, shaking her head, her drawings will not be the same.

Aba blanches at the suggestion that she could be an artist when she grows up. No, no, she protests, "I want to become a nun." To which Julie replies, "She changes her mind so fast. Last month she wanted to become a taxi driver."

Me, I just wish Aba could be a child forever.

Celebrity
November 30, 1978

Aba Dalena graduated from the University of the Philippines College of Fine Arts and is now a full-time artist. She has already had both solo and group shows. Taking after both her parents, she paints and sculpts, and is also, says her proud mother Julie, a devout Christian. Aba's ambition is to do large sculptures that will have a strong impact on the public.

Pete's Angels and Other Antiques

Petronilo Bn. Daroy is more fortunate than most people who can only dream of owning beautiful furniture and changing it as often as they wish. Daroy's house acquires a new look several times a year, and not because he's wallowing in wealth. He deals in antiques — right in his own home. Everything in the house is for sale, from the ashtrays to the teacups. He never even knows how long he will be sleeping on his bed.

Daroy's interest in antiques goes back to his years as an English major, and later an English professor, at the University of the Philippines, when the arty thing to do was to collect things of antiquity. A clerk who worked at the university — and now owns an antique shop on Mabini in Ermita — sold Ming jars and such on the side and accepted payment from students and faculty on easy installment terms. Ming jars which now fetch P200 or P300 each could be had then for P20 or P60 at most. Daroy became an avid buyer and serious collector.

His collection of antiques was not to endure, however. When martial law was imposed in 1972, Daroy, then managing editor of *Graphic Magazine,* was among the first writers to be arrested by the military. Together with his freedom he also lost his entire collection, not to mention everything else he owned — even, he moans, "my dirty underwear." The loss, though painful, was not traumatic, and today he dismisses it as "one of those things." He was detained for three and a half years, during which time he organized history, art and language classes among the other detainees. It was then that this Samareño, who speaks English with the Visayan's *malambing* accent, learned to speak Pilipino.

Once out of detention, he returned to the U.P. campus to teach and in later years, to head the English department. He needed a new place to live, but first he had to convince U.P. authorities

Petronilo Bn. Daroy

that he could afford a house on the campus. So he started buying furniture — antiques again. He got his house but could not keep his furniture for very long. Friends who were about to marry or move to a new apartment would offer to buy his stuff, at a profit to him. It was then that Daroy realized he could go into business.

Now the house is fairly brimming with the items dear to the antique collector's heart: *santos,* wall clocks, pulley lamps, candelabra, a carrara marble angel from some cemetery, chandeliers, a 1928 *Webster's International Dictionary,* teakwood chairs, camphor chests, antlers, porcelain saucers, figurines, ashtrays and plates, a silver missal holder, Sung pieces from the ninth century, a huge carved narra mirror from Balayan, Batangas. More impressive is the six-foot-tall narra door carved with the image of the Santo Niño which leans against a wall outside the house.

That is not all. In the garden behind the house is a white jar for drinking water which American colonial missionaries brought over at the turn of the century, plus Sung jars, planters, an old wooden rice thresher, even a pink baby's crib. To accommodate his sizable stock of furniture, Daroy has built a makeshift house beside his bungalow. There, restoration specialists work all day fixing beds, *aparador* and chairs. His workers can restore anything, Daroy claims, except when the material involved is teakwood or Vienna bentwood which are not available.

Adjoining the restoration workshop is Daroy's dining room/ kitchen, where he keeps an *aparador* that boasts gargoyle-shaped opium weights and plates of 22-karat gold, among other valuables. Here, too, are room dividers of colored glass and wood, actually old windows that Daroy has put together to serve a completely new purpose. An entire altar from Bulacan, its three plaster images of saints still intact, keeps Daroy sacred company when he dines. And in a small area within this room the houseboy sleeps on a brass bed, also for sale.

Where does all this great variety of antiques spring from?

From all over the country, says Daroy. While on a year's sabbatical to do research, he also went out looking for antique dealers. It is they who now knock at Daroy's door, coming from as far away as Samar and as close by as Batangas. "They know more or less my taste by now," he says. "I can't just buy anything because I don't have too much money. So I select." His preferences are "19th-century things and folk art."

Business is "quite all right," not hectic. This is, after all, just a house. Nothing, Daroy says, stays longer than six months. Even without media advertisements, he has been able to attract a regular clientele, among them friends of his whom he favors with easier payment terms. In earlier days, Daroy and his friends prepared activist-style leaflets which they handed out house-to-house in subdivisions.

Daroy corrects the impression that antiques are expensive. Not, he says, when you consider the cost of furniture these days. He should know. He and some friends have surveyed furniture stores and found that even in nonfashionable establishments things are more expensive and the materials and workmanship not as good as antique pieces. "These people," he says of the furniture makers of old, "built for function."

His prices range from P2 for a porcelain saucer to P20,000 for the Santo Niño church door. The carroza coffee table in the living room is P6,000. Daroy also has rugs he bought on a recent trip to Jeddah — Karachi rugs for P3,000, Persian rugs for P3,700, with the thicker kind costing twice as much.

DAROY'S ANTIQUES, however, do not keep him home all day. He is hardly the person that his business (called The Recluse) would suggest he is. Now that "there is not much to write," he works as director of the U.P. Information Office, which was created during the presidency of Onofre D. Corpuz, now the education minister. In the 19 years Daroy has served the university, he has worked with presidents from Dr. Vicente Sinco to Corpuz (but only for a few months) in positions that ranged from assistant to the budget director to special assistant to the president.

Daroy's teaching career had a controversial start. As a young instructor, he was nearly expelled for allegedly corrupting young minds, all because he allowed his students to read D.H. Lawrence. Today, he misses not so much teaching but the quality of students in his time. "I think the kids then had an openness, a curiosity about life. Kids now are very purposive. At that time the kids were more interested in experiment. Somehow I miss that."

He himself grew up in Catbalogan, which he describes as "a beautiful place, a seacoast town, very old; the harbor curves like Rio de Janeiro. It looks like an old Neapolitan town." The only child of teachers, he had "a very colonial education." He remembers reading Sinclair Lewis' *Main Street* and Theodore Dreiser's *American Tragedy*, and imbibing their theme of revolt against the village mentality. He wanted to get away from the small town.

He would never have been able to do that if his mother had her way. She wanted him to become a priest, but his father's will prevailed. His son, who had already displayed a flair for writing, was sent to U.P.

Daroy now views his boyhood in a new light. "I don't think," he says, "I would be as bored there now as when I was a boy. In my work I don't have to kowtow to power. I can always go back to Samar and plant *kamote.*"

That kind of detachment from the goods of this earth, be they power or possessions, characterizes Daroy's attitude towards his antiques as well. For while he keeps a splendid collection of angels for himself, everything else to him is dispensable. "I never had," he says, "a love for possessions for their own sake." A great deal of this detachment was learned not only in childhood but also in his days as an activist. "I derived a lot of sense from the movement," he says, not the least of which is the conviction that "I will not allow property to overpower me, to possess me."

Celebrity
December 15, 1981

Pete Daroy moved out of the U.P. campus after his retirement and bought himself a farm in Bustos, Bulacan. He continued to sell antiques, but took as much pride in his thriving mango trees. In recent years, he added vintage cars to his sales catalogue. In the early Nineties, he suffered a stroke from which he never fully recovered. He died following a heart attack on January 26, 2000. He was a journalist till the end, writing a regular column for the Sun-Star Daily.

Nora Daza on TV

Nora Villanueva Daza, Supercook, is as unflappable off camera as she is on it. Here she is on taping day for *Cooking It Up With Nora*, of which she is both star and producer, and she never once loses her cool even though this is her third show for the day and there is one more to go. The eyes, framed by bluish-grey eye shadow, are bright and warm. The voice is cheerful, and the "please" and "thank you" for assistants and crew are never missing.

I had never seen her before except on television, where I have been watching her on and off through all the years she's been cooking on the tube; in magazines and newspapers, where not only her recipes but also her personal life has made good copy; and on the back cover of her cookbook, which my husband, exasperated with my feeble attempts in the kitchen, brought home one evening years ago.

The lady cuts a striking figure on the set. No longer as slim as she was, say 10 years ago, but still statuesque, she moves elegantly even among pots and pans and Tupperware containers. And the elegance comes not just from the dress she is wearing. Her production assistant, a young woman named Hazel, whispers that the dress came from Paris, to which Ms. Daza commutes as casually as lesser mortals do Quiapo and Divisoria. It is a black chiffon gown she has on, with pink birds and grey clouds, and when she stands under the lights, the diaphanous quality of the material affords a glimpse of legs that are long and slim.

On the set Nora Daza is queen of a kitchen that is wallpapered in green and white and adequately stocked with the products of Filipro, Liberty Flour Mills, Ajinomoto and other show sponsors. There is a green Wynner refrigerator on the right side, and the thoroughly professional Ms. Daza constantly plugs Wynner in her spiels.

Nora V. Daza

Now she is interviewing Robert Kuan, president of the newly launched Ling Nam Dimsum Palace atop Au Bon Vivant in Makati, and expounding on the merits of the suckling pig in front of them, which Ling Nam's Chinese chef has lit up with battery-operated bulbs inserted in flower-shaped *singkamas*. In a little while, Ms. Daza will be sitting down with Rita Van Der Sheer and her six-year-old Saskia and, over glasses of eggnog, they will be reliving Christmas in Holland. The rest of the hour Ms. Daza will be showing the ladies at home how to make desserts and special dishes for the Christmas holidays. She will be breezing through it all without benefit of script or cue cards.

"Everybody thinks it's easy," she says with a sigh between sips of Coke at break-time. "Do you know that after doing a show, I'm drained. I don't have a script, it's all in my head and I want to do it well. Sometimes when I do a bad show—like when the recipes don't come out right — I really suffer inside. But I want people to know that I know I'm not infallible. I know that I'm no cooking expert, maybe just a little bit better than many people because I've been exposed to it and it's become my profession."

BY MOST PEOPLE'S standards, of course, Nora Daza is *the* cooking expert. And the wonder of it all is, cooking is not the only thing she does well. I have to refer to the text on the back cover of her cookbook:

"*To the saying that the world is a stage, Nora Daza adds: Life is a meal.*

"*Live it with flavor, spice it with interest in people, places and things, serve it with a feast of color, and life becomes full and rich.*

"*Her basic philosophy of making life useful and flavorful has guided her through a checkerboard of careers: From conducting a column in a women's magazine to starring for eight years on a television show for housewives, from civic duties in helping boost tourism to her private world of bowling, hunting, fishing, horseback riding, reading, writing and entertaining friends, she shows her zest for living in a variety of ways.*"

The "zest for living" is, as everybody knows, most evident in her interest in good food. She has four restaurants in Manila alone to prove that, a fifth in Paris and a sixth in New York. The pity is that she has not much time these days to cook.

"I used to cook a lot. I've been telling myself I have to find time to cook. I'm running four restaurants, plus there are my children. I don't even have time for a social life. And I travel. But I must cook. If you don't cook, you lose the touch. When I'm organizing a restaurant, then I cook. The last time I did that was with Galing-Galing. Now I just tell my staff to do this, do that, instead of doing it myself. I'm like an executive chef. Sometimes I tell myself I'm going to do this because I see something and I feel I can do it better, not because I understand how ingredients work."

She has been walking around the set in sleek black shoes with five-inch heels. Now she is taking them off and slipping her feet into black "Jourdan-designed" slippers before she takes her place behind the demonstration table to start her cooking lessons. There are thousands of women who swear by Nora Daza's recipes, who say that even without formal lessons they have learned to cook by simply following her instructions to the last pinch of pepper. She is that good, according to her legion of disciples.

But the afternoon is turning out to be one of those bad times. The oil in the pan, meant for deep-frying apple slices the Dutch way, is splattering madly: there's water in the oil, Supercook declares. The gelatin for another recipe did not form. "Sometimes it happens," she tells her viewers as she flashes that dazzling smile again.

There are minor irritants. She holds up the strainer and mutters to her assistant, *"Wala bang maganda-gandang* strainer? *Puwede ba, bumili ka ng magandang* strainer?" And then, failing to find a knife she needs, she frowns, *"Wala na ba tayong kutsilyo?* I brought knives back from Paris." But the dazzling smile is back on her face in seconds, even when she sees flies around the table. "She keeps her cool most of the time," says Hazel.

The third show is almost over. It is to be the Christmas Eve program and Nora Daza feels she should have changed into another dress. Gigi Calero, her director, assures her people won't notice, The two shows in which she is wearing the same dress won't be shown on consecutive Sundays anyway. Ms. Daza leaves the matter at that. I suppose when someone is as lovely as she is, viewers really wouldn't raise a fuss over her wardrobe.

By now, one of her male assistants is squatting on the floor beside the long table and washing a pile of dirty dishes and bowls and cutlery in a pail of water. He should be packing up in about two hours. Ms. Daza's personal maid, a young girl who wears a thick braid down to her buttocks, is still standing by patiently. She has been doing that since this morning.

As I leave the set, the last thing I see is the pair of sleek black shoes, lying now beside the Wynner refrigerator. It has been an exhausting day.

Celebrity
December 15, 1978

Nora V. Daza lives in Paris where she runs a Filipino restaurant called Aux Iles Philippines. It is, she says, her way of doing some good for her country. Having turned 70 in December 1998, she is planning her "ultimate cookbook," her last one, as she "may finally go into my own type of retirement." She is happy that all her children are more or less settled and proud to have 15 (going on 16) very bright grandchildren." In December 1998 she e-mailed from Paris: "My children and grandchildren are the sum total of a very full, wonderful life, and I'm not including my love life yet... God has been so good to me for I have had a fantastically full, interesting and blessed life." That includes introducing foreign cuisine in the Philippines and high-end Philippine restaurants in Europe and New York City, and even an unsuccessful run for the Senate in 1992 at the invitation of the Nacionalista Party. Her cookbook, Let's Cook with Nora, *is still the bible of Philippine cuisine.*

On His Way to the Top, I Met Gang Gomez

The first time I wrote about a fashion designer in this space, I found out that what plagues the local fashion industry is not lack of government support, not the inferior quality of Philippine textiles, not the parochial taste of the Filipino public, but pettiness and envy. I was appalled to discover that despite their supposedly hectic professional lives, there are those in the industry who delight in nitpicking, in scrutinizing magazine stories word for word and then reading into them the meaning that is not there, and finally raising a howl over an imagined insult. I swore to myself I would not make the same mistake again. That is, write about another fashion designer.

But Gang Gomez is different, says someone who is trying to talk me into writing about him. A nice sort of person, insists this friend who has known Gomez for years. Aren't they all when they're starting out, I tell myself. Anyhow, to please Gang's friend and mine, I go and see for myself.

Gang Gomez makes his appearance smelling fragrant, looking fair and boyish and wholesome, like some kind of refined, well-bred *colegiala* in a dog-eat-dog world, if he will pardon the comparison. He speaks breathlessly and excitedly, his English almost flawless, and all the while, as he talks, his eyes and lips smile. I wonder how long he can keep that up, but he does for almost two hours.

There is a world of difference between him and his colleagues. I mean, how many fashion designers have a bachelor's degree in philosophy, cum laude, to their name, and the whole caboodle of units for a master's in philosophy, to boot? Because that's what Gomez has, in addition to solid training in one of New York's top fashion schools.

GANG GOMEZ

Not even his mother can remember how Edgardo Ramon became Gang, but that has been his nickname ever since he can remember, and not, as some people surmise, only since he became a fashion designer. He graduated from a high school in Pampanga at 14, too young to go to New York and enroll in a fashion course, which was what he had wanted to do all along. Mother said no, a liberal arts course in Manila should be better. She had hoped fashion would be just a passing fancy to her son. Gang went to San Beda, finding himself working hard because an older brother had graduated years earlier as high school valedictorian, and being rewarded for his efforts with a cum laude. *Kulelat* among the honor graduates, he says with a sheepish smile. The dean at San Beda, informed by the earnest young man that after his A.B. he would go into fashion design, was not ecstatic.

Mother decreed he was still too young, at 18, to go to New York all by himself, but by this time she had resigned herself to the fact that fashion, to her younger son, was no passing fancy. Gang had time on his hands while waiting to grow old enough for New York, and kept himself busy at the graduate school of the University of Santo Tomas and at Slim's Fashion School. He took all his masteral units in philosophy in two years, at the end of which it was his turn to tell his parents, "I'm 20 and I think I'm too young to write my thesis." How, he asked them, could he be expected to write his philosophy of life at 20? He begged them to let him go to New York. They relented, but only after he assured them that he would read up on philosophy in his free time and start working on his thesis. "As it turned out," says Gang happily, "I finished all my designing classes and forgot about my philosophical readings."

He breezed through his classes at Mayers School of Fashion Design, winning, at the end of the course, the right to represent the school in the prestigious training course cum competition of the New York Fashion Designers Foundation, for which only the top students of the city's best fashion schools are qualified. The training was rigorous and first-rate. Students submitted fashion sketches which had to be approved by a board of judges, worked on their patterns right in front of the board, then did the sewing themselves. Gang values the experience highly. "Here in our country," he says, "the designer is only a sketcher. In every fashion capital of the world, a designer is someone who not only draws but also cuts, drapes, sews. One has to know the basics of construction."

The climax of the competition was a fashion show in which all the remaining students were to display their gowns. Gang's entry — an all-black evening jumpsuit of classic French lace lightly traced with beadwork, over which the model wore a black silk chiffon cape — won the top prize. He likes to believe luck was on his side that evening. He had the right fabrics, his model was a favorite of the designer Valentino, and the week before the show all of New York's trendsetter stores — Saks, Bergdorf Goodman, Lord and Taylor — had decreed, through their show windows, that black was the color of the season.

The prizewinning gown, with its Muslim keyhole neckline, is now stored in the museum-library of the New York Fashion Foundation, along with all the other winners of the annual competition. Gang has yet to make a nostalgic trip to the museum, never having had the time to do so on two subsequent visits to New York to stage fashion shows at the Philippine Center.

SINCE COMING home in 1971, Gang has been burying himself in work, first as a designer for Christian Espiritu and three years later, as his own boss. Christian still calls him the most professional of all the assistants he has had — and there have been many — and Gang himself is the first to tell you that when he accepted the job, he stipulated to Christian that he would be thoroughly professional. He kept regular working hours, but also stayed in the shop supervising the workers till midnight or the early morning hours when gowns had to be rushed.

It is a pace he keeps even today. "My attitude until now," he says, "is that the things I can do, I do by myself. You'll never see me sitting down doing nothing. In the evening, when I have nothing to do, I work. I can drape until midnight. When there's beading to be finished, I help out till 2 a.m. I don't think anything is beneath my dignity to do."

That is why Gang Gomez has no time for any of the intrigues and petty jealousies which wrack his profession. He calls himself neutral ground, Switzerland, for the many bickering sets of designers. "I have always," he says, "maintained a certain distance. I'm very friendly with all my colleagues but I keep my distance. It works very well for me." Except for Barge Ramos, Gang's circle of close friends does not include designers.

Gang is giving himself another five years to make the big time. He is, he says, "going very slowly, but very surely." His is a small clientele, limited, as he puts it, to mature women who know what they want and are willing to spend for it. With his reputation for classic, neat and uncluttered lines, he feels happy about the return of the shape to women's fashion and predicts that "a few of the designers who made it in the past two years, when the biggie was in, will have to try harder or get pushed out of the rat race."

Gang turned 31 a fortnight ago. I'd like to see him again five years from now. Will he still be Switzerland then?

Celebrity
June 30, 1979

Gang Gomez gave up his fashion designing career in 1989, after 17 successful years, and entered the Monastery of the Transfiguration in San Jose, Malaybalay, Bukidnon. To the surprise of his friends, he adapted easily to the monastic life and took his final vows as Dom Martin de Jesus Gomez in December 1996. His artistic talent, however, has not been completely lost to the outside world. In 1997 he began research on indigenous and local materials to see how these could be put to use in liturgical vestments. The result of his research was a widely praised exhibition of Filipino liturgical vestments at the Ayala Museum, his unique contribution to the celebration of the centennial of Philippine independence. He is writing a coffee-table book based on the exhibition, to be published by the Ayala Museum.

Cecile Guidote's Dreams for Theatre

Cecile Guidote is PETA and PETA is Cecile Guidote. She would be the first to protest this simplification of her role in the success of the Philippine Educational Theatre Association, but that is just like her. The fact is that PETA would never have been if an 18-year-old Paulinian back in 1962 had not dreamed the great dream of a national theatre for the Philippines, not unlike those in Europe, the United States, and even Korea.

Determination is not one of Cecile's virtues for nothing. After graduating from St. Paul College and being named one of the country's Ten Outstanding Students, she applied for a Rockefeller grant to the Dallas Theatre Center in Texas and got it. Her thesis at the end of the course was titled "Prospectus for the National Theatre of the Philippines," a 300-page work which, when actualized, was to become PETA.

Cecile came home in January 1967 and wasted no time contacting the right people for her project. The three organizations which she approached for support — the National Office of Radio and Television, the Citizens Council for Mass Media and Unesco, Philippines — were enthusiastic. Like Cecile, they were convinced that if theatre arts were to grow in this country and assume a significant role "in the cultural growth and educational experience of our citizens," there was need to coordinate the activities of school and community drama groups and enlist the support of private patrons, institutions, government bodies and professional organizations concerned with the arts.

In barely five years, PETA has become synonymous with excellence in the theatre and television drama. At Fort Santiago, PETA's Rajah Sulayman Theatre offers a regular season of plays in

CECILE GUIDOTE

both English and Pilipino. The productions have ranged from Nick Joaquin's *Larawan* to Paul Dumol's *Paglilitis ni Mang Serapio* to *Ang Tao*, the Pilipino adaptation of *Everyman*. A more recent activity at Fort Santiago was the playwrights' development program which enabled playwrights who had never seen their plays onstage to test the work and gauge audience reactions. The program has tapped very young talents, of whom Cecile is justifiably proud.

Equally well known are PETA's achievements in television. *Balintataw* has won the Citizens Award for Television (CAT) for best dramatic anthology four times, for best television director (Lupita A. Concio) twice, and for best scriptwriting twice. Cecile's brief remarks when she accepted the 1970 CAT award for best dramatic anthology are worth remembering:

"We are happy for this award as an affirmation of our conviction that television is not just a commercial industry but that the medium drawing imaginatively from theatre resources is indeed an art and a unique social force bringing meaningful cultural experience to Filipinos through a relevant interpretation of life that affects our beliefs, habits, emotional attitudes and values.

"This award which we have now enjoyed for the fourth year strengthens our commitment to promote professionalism and to creatively apply the Dramatic Arts as an effective instrument in forging our people's cultural identity and advancing our country's national development."

Timed for the opening of the Constitutional Convention is a series of socially relevant plays for television aimed at "politicizing the masses through dramatic arts." In addition, *Balintataw* will present monthly, starting in April, a historical drama with the cooperation of the National Historical Commission.

For Cecile, time is of the essence. Through the Central Institute of Theatre Arts in the Philippines (CITAP), she hopes to bring about a unique theatrical form from a synthesis of Asian practices and Western technology. "We know London and Broadway plays better than we do Vietnamese theatre," she moans.

Soon, Cecile hopes, PETA will be able to branch out into film. With its pool of talented actors, actresses, directors and scriptwriters, PETA could revolutionize the Filipino movie industry.

THE WONDER OF PETA is that it has been able to function on a shoestring budget. No, says Cecile, the government has not lent a hand, although a bill is now pending in Congress which provides for the integration of creative dramatics in the curriculum as well as for the creation of a division of arts in the Department of Education.

From the First Lady the only concrete forms of support have been scholarships in the PETA summer theatre classes last year for out-of-school youth. A lump sum subsidy appears to be too much to ask for. There have been helpful friends, though. Like Teodoro Valencia, UNESCO, Goethe House, the Asia and Rockefeller Foundations. The latter is sponsoring the visit here this summer of awardwinning American director Brooks Jones, who will conduct a two-month video-film workshop. Cecile says, "The trouble with the government is that it has not realized that the arts have a place in our country. What we want to show is that theatre has a part in national development. Once this fact is recognized, then we will find a place for PETA in government funds."

One hopes, for our country's sake, that the government will see its way to supporting PETA in time for the Afro-Arabic Asian Theatre Arts Festival and International Conference from November 19 to 30 this year. The projected festival will coincide with the celebration of Manila's 400th year.

CECILE HAD DREAMED of becoming a lawyer. "I always wanted to be in public service, but not as a politician. When I got to college and became more deeply involved in drama as a form of public service, I realized the potency of drama. I could see the force for change that drama could be. And I knew I had to work for a national theatre movement and put it on par with the international movement."

Late last month, at PETA's fifth national theatre convention, brighter hopes were raised for theatre in the country. Heherson Alvarez, delegate-elect from Isabela to the Constitutional Convention, heard proposals on arts and culture for the new constitution and led discussions on how cooperative drama projects could politicize the masses. Also discussed was the application of creative theatre principles for the social rehabilitation of the physically handicapped, the mentally retarded, prisoners and out-of-school youth.

It has been an uphill struggle for Cecile Guidote. The rewards have been great, but the credit, she will hastily explain, is not hers alone. The girl is like that. It is difficult to get her to talk about herself, but not about PETA.

"It's a good investment to train people but they must be people with commitment. Training cannot be just talent and ego," she declares.

Can one imagine PETA without Cecile?

"The company is growing and so many people have been trained to take over." It is her way of saying that the deadline she had set for herself at the start of PETA — five years of total commitment — is nearing. And that, hopefully, she can think of marriage.

But between that time and now, there are the Teen Theatre League, the workers' theatre, *Balintataw*, Raha Sulayman, the November festival and countless other commitments that all spell PETA to fill her days.

Asia-Philippines Leader
April 9, 1971

Cecile Guidote is no longer connected with PETA, but her vision for it has been nurtured and expanded over the years by young people who also believe in the power of people's theatre. Cecile was forced to leave the country in 1971 when her husband, Heherson T. Alvarez, had to go into exile in the United States to escape a shoot-to-kill order from the Marcos regime. The Alvarezes lived in exile in the United States for 13 years during the Marcos dictatorship, returning to the Philippines with their two children only after the EDSA people power revolt. While in exile, the couple worked actively in the Movement for a Free Philippines and the Ninoy Aquino Movement. Cecile continued to be involved in theatre while in the U.S., but focused on human rights and peace. She has founded various organizations that espouse human rights, disarmament, children's rights and the environment. Among these organizations are the International Alliance of Concerned Artists for Human Rights and Peace, International League of Folk Arts for Communications and Education, and DREAMS Academy. She hosts and produces a drama series, "Balintataw," for television and radio. As artistic and training director of the Earthsavers-DREAMS Academy at the Ninoy Aquino Park in Quezon City, she provides cultural and livelihood studies for street children, and ethnic and disabled youth. She was appointed UNESCO commissioner during the Aquino and Ramos administrations. Her work on various causes has earned for her a number of awards and citations here and abroad. Her husband, a former senator, now represents Isabela in the House of Representatives.

HILDA KORONEL
Off the Cuff

"But I'm such a big, fat pig," she protested when the idea of a *Celebrity* interview was first broached to her. She was deep in rehearsals for Nick Joaquin's *Mga Ama, Mga Anak,* where she was playing her first stage role, and I had gone to see her at Philamlife Auditorium one evening. She did look much heavier than she does in the Lux commercial, particularly around the waist and hips, but otherwise she looked gorgeous.

Hilda Koronel went out of circulation soon after making her first supposedly bold movie, *Hayop sa Hayop,* and soon after rumors floated about her reconciliation with one-time beau Jay Ilagan. There were more subsequent rumors and nasty gossip in the movie press — about a pregnancy, which was confirmed in June this year by news of the birth of a baby girl.

I had intimations about the state of affairs in the Koronel and Ilagan households when I called up the Ilagan home at about that time to arrange for an interview with Jay Ilagan. A little girl volunteered the information that *"Ay, hindi na dito nakatira si Tito Jay, kina Tita Susan na,"* although a male voice promptly took over the phone to correct whatever wrong impression the little girl may have conveyed. Not true, he said, sounding flustered, Jay was staying in his own home. I had been calling the Ilagan house many times before then and had spoken to the actor's mother often enough to recognize her voice anywhere. I was positive it was the same voice I heard when I called Hilda Koronel's home three months later, but not wanting to seem too forward, I had desisted from asking the older woman if she was indeed Mrs. Ilagan. She saved me the trouble, however, by identifying herself. But the next time I called and, as per her instructions the day before, asked for Mrs. Ilagan, I was told, *"Aling* Mrs. Ilagan?" *Aha,* I thought, so there are two Mrs. Ilagans. I asked for the older Mrs. Ilagan.

HILDA KORONEL

Hilda Koronel lives in a Spanish-style house near the end of a Cubao street that is lined with apartments and unpretentious-looking homes. There is no doorbell at her gate and it is a long time before anyone opens the door, so I have time to, as they say, case the joint. A black MSR Manta with seats upholstered in black and white checks is parked in the driveway. Among the clothes hanging in the driveway to dry, I make out red jogging pants and black leotards.

After about 10 minutes the first head, a boy's, pops out of a side door. He promptly puts his head back in. Then a woman comes out, takes a look at me and disappears. Nothing happens. A middle-aged woman in a white uniform, perhaps a *yaya*, comes towards the gate but she only wants to check whether the clothes on the line are dry. Noticing me, she asks what my business is. Then she enters the house and the first woman comes out again and invites me inside.

The living room is incredibly tidy; the granolithic flooring looks unstepped on. I sense a conscious effort to carry over to the house's interior design the Spanish influence of its exterior. There are two sala sets: one, heavy and richly carved and upholstered in deep red; the other, a more cozy set in moss green. There is a profusion of blown-glass floral and fruit arrangements on the marble tables and a huge plastic potted plant stands at the archway leading to the dining room. I wonder, with all the children whose voices I now hear, how the house could be kept so neat.

The children — there must be four or five of them — look at me curiously as I sit on the green sofa. Two pretty little girls take turns peering at me and then look at each other amusedly. A curly-topped little mestizo is not so friendly: he leers at me from the top of the stairs and makes faces and then blurts out, *"Galit kita, punta-punta ka pa dito."*

Hilda Koronel finally comes down wearing a flowered housedress in ice blue and oversized green and white bedroom slippers. I can't help noticing several deep lines around her neck, the kind that overweight during pregnancy can bring about. She says she weighed 188 pounds just before her delivery and, thanks to almost daily workouts at the Mandarin's Hatch and Reed gym and squash and tennis and a strict diet, she is now down to 130, which is still 20 pounds in excess of her normal weight. Hatch and Reed is "very effective, but it's up to the person really. If you don't put your heart in it, it won't work. I think in anything it is like that."

I am to find out, as the interview progresses, that that statement might as well explain Hilda Koronel's astounding self-development not only as an actress but also as a woman. Eight years ago, I passed up a chance to interview her, then Lea Productions' hottest property, for a national publication. Interviewing Nora Aunor and Vilma Santos had been ordeals in themselves and so, when my editor suggested I do Hilda next, I said no thank you, without a second thought. I was not sorry I declined the assignment. The writer who eventually took it came back to the office after interviewing Hilda, spewing invectives because the 14-year-old Lea star had only one word in her vocabulary: "okay." It was all the girl could answer, Ninotchka Rosca fumed.

Today, Hilda Koronel, way past her Lea years, has blossomed into a very articulate and self-possessed young woman with a mind and a will of her own. At Maryknoll College, where she is an international studies senior, the teachers concede that she has "a good mind" and regret that her energies have to be dissipated in so many activities. Hilda herself says that if she had all the time in the world, school would be so easy.

In this very candid interview, Hilda Koronel, who is known to be a very private person, speaks of her film career, the movie industry, school, the men in her life, Jay Ilagan and her children, including three-month-old Leona Paula, who has "her Papa's eyes."

Where does Hilda Koronel end and Susan Reid begin?

I know where my Hilda Koronel ends and where my Susan Reid starts. My private life is really Susan. I give the public just a little part of me. Of course, they're used to Hilda Koronel. When I was just starting and people would call me Hilda, *hindi ko maalala*. Even in school nobody calls me Hilda, nobody. I feel I'm a person there, *hindi* idol. I forbid it. Even my checkbooks carry the name Susan Reid. *Sa* movies *lang talaga ang* Hilda. But even my movie friends call me Susan. When I call the parlor for an appointment, I use Susan. *Sanay lang ang* public *na konti lang* Hilda Koronel *ang alam*. I really treasure my privacy. I keep a dividing line.

Which is why people say you're a snob.
Yes, but that's not true. I give them only up to a certain point. Otherwise the whole system will swallow me up. That's what I was telling Lloyd (Samartino, her co-star in Nick Joaquin's *Mga Ama, Mga Anak*). Lino and I and the rest of the cast were telling Lloyd about the star system, that you have to put up with a lot of things if you're a newcomer. And I said, *Hala,* if you're not strong, they'll just swallow you up and you become a part of the system and then you're nothing afterward. *Dinaanan din namin.*

You started in the movies at 14?
No, I started when I was 12 in 1969. I didn't get into the movies through "Nightowl Dance Party." We had relatives in Channel 11. I started in "Nightowl" when I was seven, eight, and every year I would win. I won second in the finals. Jessica (the former *bomba* star) was first. I was well developed at an early age. It was fun winning. After a while I stopped. Then we had a friend who headed a recruiting office for extras. We usually went to the studios to watch shootings. Once we went to LVN looking for this woman and a film editor saw me. He asked if I wanted to be in the movies. I said yes, out of curiosity, and he took me to Lea, where they shot my picture. The following week I was in a film. It was fast, there was no time to think about it. *Matagal na din iyon* — 10 years. *Siyempre,* when I was young, *halo-halo ang* views, ideas. My guiding factor was Lino (Brocka). I met him when I was 18. When I was 13, 14, I didn't know I was making mistakes. I would do taping, I was so young, *ang mga tao nasasaktan ko pala* but I didn't know and he would come to me and say this is wrong. He would explain and I would cry *kasi hindi ko naman sinasadya.* So eventually I realized *ito tama, ito hindi.* He was setting *parang* guidelines, this is what you should do. *Parang nandoon na ang* structure, but he was guiding me along that line. He was a father, a brother, a friend, everything. *Parang* we grew up together in the

movies *kasi sabay ang* discovery *namin sa* Lea, and then as persons. Maybe he saw the potential.

Where did you grow up?

In Manila. I grew up with my Mom's sister in a very violent place in Pasay. There were gang wars. The environment was not very good. That's why my friends ask how come I was not psychologically affected by my environment. Usually, *hindi ba,* they say you are what your environment is. But what happened to me is the opposite. I don't know how I was able to distinguish right from wrong at the time. The people I grew up with had different ideas and opinions from me. My uncle was very strict—black was black, you couldn't argue. Go to church every day, you could not look at boys, that was a sin. I told myself I couldn't let my own children grow up that way. My friends say *dapat naging ganoon din ako.* But I don't understand why I turned out this way. No one was guiding me. I didn't see my father that much. Then he and my mother split up. So most of my life I had no father. But I'm not bitter. *Hindi naman ako lumaking masama. Wala akong* hang-ups.

How many movies have you made?

Ang dami-dami na. I don't remember. My first movie was a screen test, *Leslie* with Boots and Liza. After that, *tuloy-tuloy na.* Maybe it was fate. It all happened so fast. They asked me, you want to be an actress. *Tapos,* screen test. *Tapos,* starring role *na.*

But you always wanted to be a movie star.

No. But when I was small, people always told me, "*A, mag-aartista ang batang ito paglaki niya.*" Me, because *laging inuulit sa akin,* I hated the idea. *Wala akong hilig umarte.* There were plays in school and every year, Santacruzan *sagala,* but I hated it. I entered the movies out of curiosity.

You were advanced for your age.

Yes, I was. When I was young, 12, I had the mind of a 17-year-old. Now I feel 30-plus, 40. That's why when I was 19, I couldn't date boys my age. Even now, when I was separated before, I couldn't date boys my age because my mind was so far advanced, more mature, *hindi kami nagkakaintindihan*. They were young, fun-loving, they loved to dance, my mind was somewhere else. I love to read books and I like to discuss things I read, the movies, a little of everything, and you can do this only with an older person. I would go out with men — not 40s, DOM *na iyon*. When I was 19, I would go out with men *mga* 28, 33. The youngest I went out with was 27 or 26. The best age gap for me was about 14 years. They knew how to treat women and *magandang kausap. Mahilig din akong sumayaw* but I can't do it every night. I wanted something deeper — marijuana, drink, they all end, *hanggang doon na lang*. There must be something beyond those.

What role affected you most deeply?

Maybe Insiang. It was a very good role, it was really made for me. I did it on television when I was much younger and Lino thought it would be a good vehicle when I reached a certain age of maturity. I think I was 14 when I did it. He said I was not mature enough then — *hindi pa kaya sa* character, *hindi pa masyadong* developed. He promised me when I got to be 18 he would do a movie for me, really for me.

With what role did you identify most?

With dramatic roles in general. When you mention my name, people think of that.

Which role has given you fulfillment in terms of performance?

Dramatic roles. During my Lea days I used to do comedies *pero hindi maganda*. I feel I can do them too but they have to be done well. My sense of humor is different — not the Dolphy type, but *siguro Mang* Nano type. Maybe sarcastic.

I did not see *Hayop sa Hayop*...

Neither did I. I was in KL as a film festival delegate. When I arrived, *wala na*. Yes, in a way, I feel I've missed something when I don't see my movies. *Pero wala akong magagawa. Pero pag alam kong pangit ang* movie, I really don't see it. It's frustrating. *Siyempre minsan hindi mo maiwasan* — you get a good script but the director is not so good. *Siyempre hindi mo naman alam,* you have to give everybody a chance, and it's also work. And then you find out *hindi mahusay ang* director so *hindi maganda ang* execution *ng* movie.

I saw stills of *Hayop sa Hayop* that showed you in the nude.
Supposed to be. Did you see the one in *Expressweek*? The pictorials were much more bold than the movie. In the movie it was just my back that was seen, so people said *harang*. I was wearing a bikini. I took off the top and I was submerged in water and sitting on a rock. Then there was a waterfall overhead. Then the kissing scene. That was all. The bikini top had to go at the end because *nakikita pa rin*. So we taped my breasts and I was covering them with my arms. I never let go *kahit nagsasabon. Ang tagal naming ginawa iyon.*

Ang daming offers after that movie, about 13 offers for bold movies. *Iyong iba maganda ang* story, *pero takot ako sa* director. *Hayop* I did because of Lino. Otherwise I wouldn't have done it. I'm too scared *sa ibang* director, *nagsasamantala*. With Lino, I'm not scared. I'm willing to work with other directors, but I'm very cautious. I ask for the script and I mark the parts that are questionable. We discuss. We do it in a contract, to be safe. I say, *ano ba itong eksenang ito,* I cannot do things like this. And I talk to the director.

How did you develop yourself as an actress?
My training ground was television and there again it was with Lino. I had no formal training. My TV show. *Hilda,* was a weekly thing and ran for almost five years. Every week it was a different role. Lino would teach me body movements, that by doing things with my hand I could convey certain emotions, even tension, in a scene. He would explain it to me piece by piece until I got it.

Movies I watch for enjoyment. *Kunyari* a Glenda Jackson movie — she's really a fantastic actress. I notice her acting but I don't copy technique. I don't dissect movies because then I wouldn't enjoy them. *Dito sa atin kailangan maganda ka muna, hindi kailangang marunong umarte.*

Why did you leave Lea?

When my five-year contract was about to expire, I couldn't stand it anymore. They were leading my life for me, *'yung* dates *mo sila ang mamimili*. I couldn't go out *kung hindi naka*-makeup *kasi ganoon daw dapat ang artista*. You couldn't blame them — that was their concept of a movie star then. You had to look stunning, you had to be nice, *at marami pang* reasons, personal reasons.

It was not easy leaving them. I had learned to love Mrs. (Emilia) Blas — I have a certain respect for her and Miss Santos — *parang magulang ko na pero magulang na mahigpit*. I was living with them, together with my mother. They were training me in the wrong way — I was growing up and I realized something was wrong with my life. I was learning to be dependent. So we talked about it. For almost a year I did not have work. They said they would allow me to make movies for other companies *pero sila ang makikipag-usap* as producer. But Lino was always there to help *kasi siyempre hirap na hirap kami*.

Then, after the contract, it was like starting again. *Parang bagong pasok na naman sa pelikula, parang* you had leprosy, nobody wanted to touch you. I got that feeling. *Kasi siyempre* producer *sina* Mrs. Blas. Then, after a while, *siguro sa tiyaga lang*, freelancing. Movies were hard to come by *noon*. Lino would help, at first with bit parts in his movies. It was slow work, but I got there.

At least now I'm stable — I'm not up, I'm not down. That's the position I want. I've proved my point. It was a big thing; I worked hard for it. Now they respect me *kahit papano*. *Pag ako ang kausap they respect me at alam nila kung sino ang kausap nila*. They know how to treat me, *hindi katulad noong araw*. They're very careful with me. I'm very nice to them, but *iyong* niceness ko *lang, hindi na ako puwedeng sumobra doon*.

What is your asking price per film today?

When I left off last year, it was already P110,000. *Nung bumalik ako ngayon* I'm asking for the same thing. Some producers say *bakit naman, e matagal kang nawala*. I don't think that should make a difference. And for that price I'm not doing any bold scene.

What do you think of the local film industry?
I don't go to social functions and parties. I don't enjoy them. *Hindi naman ako nagmamalaki pero* there's a lot of hypocrisy. I can only stand some people, *iyong mga nakakausap ko,* but the others I cannot stand. I am basically that kind of person — I cannot talk to people I don't like. *Hindi nila nakikita ang* real value. I hate it when people are nice to me but when I turn my back *titirahin ako.*

When I was much younger, in Lea, it was like that. I was taught *kailangang lahat ng pangalan ng* reporter *alam mo, lahat sila babatiin mo pag nakita mo,* you have to be nice, *Kuya* like this. I hated it. I used to do it because I was under contract. I have friends in the movie industry, including writers, but I don't go beyond...*oy,* like this, like that, making *tsismis* and all. *Parang* hypocrite *ka na rin. Kaya sinasabi nila ang suplada ko daw. Kung minsan nahihiya naman ako kaya hindi ako kumikibo,* but I say hello. I think that's enough. You don't have to make *arte* which you don't mean *naman.*

Meron diyan mga reporters, *grabe ang pagkabakla, lalapitan ka, oy, ineng, balita ko,* etc. etc., *aasarin ka.* I hate that kind of talk. If someone talks to me sensibly, *kahit ano ang gusto mong itanong, sasagutin ko.* When I give my opinions, I'm very blunt. Some misinterpret what I say, so *masasaktan naman ang mga kasama ko.* I don't want to do that. I just want to be myself. Hilda and Susan are one and the same person. Maybe some people in the movies think I'm *mayabang kasi hindi ako nakikihalo.* Why should I go somewhere if I don't enjoy myself?

Are you aspiring for superstardom?
No, not superstardom. *Maraming sakit ng ulo.* And you have to do so many dumb things which I cannot swallow because before I do something I have to think first — is it logical, is it reasonable? I don't have a manager. I hired Boy de Guia as PR only because after *Hayop, medyo marami ng* offers so Lino said I need someone at least to schedule pictorials. But as for managing my own affairs. I do that myself. I tell Boy to schedule, *hindi siya ang magsasabi.* That's why they don't control me. Nobody can run my life for me.

Do you keep an *alalay*?

I have an *alalay*. *Hindi mo maiiwasan kasi marami kang gamit.* She's been with me for years and when we have no shooting she works at home. I don't like fans coming here. They used to. I would go out, sign autographs and then go inside. I don't let them stay here.

I've done certain things *na hindi magawa ng* superstars. Nobody dared — *ako pumipili kung sino ang kakausapin ko.* I can say things I want to say. At first *medyo naiinis sila,* but I got away with all these things.

Maybe I was getting few offers for a while partly because of the image I created, partly because, especially when it comes to movies, it's hard to talk to me. *Hindi mo ako pwedeng lokohin. Kaya nahihirapan ang mga* producers *makipag-usap. Tatawaran ka pa.* When I give you my price, that's it. I won't give you a certain amount to give you a chance *na makatawad.* And when I say something, I do it. And when I say no, *kasi alanganin ako, ayoko talaga dahil ayokong mapahiya.*

How important is acting to you?

It's very important. I love doing movies but the industry is so frustrating now. The income is okey but only up to a certain time. *Malalaos ka rin,* you have to be practical. And this is a very ungrateful business. I hate to see the day *na* like *iyong nakikita kong* old stars, still working but subordinate *sa mga* superstars and they would wait. *Ayokong maging ganoon.* That's why I want another career for myself, so *kung medyo alanganin na ako sa* movies and they don't make good movies anymore, and Lino's not there anymore, I guess I'll concentrate on something else. I've been asked why I didn't take mass communication. But I know that already. I may not know the theories but I know how it works.

How are you doing in school?

I'm doing very well. If I had all the time in the world, school would be very easy.

I really enjoy school and the competition is there all the time. I really love to study. *Sa* movies, *alam mong marunong ka. Sa* school, you get zeros, *minsan hindi ka makasagot, natatalo ka* once in a while *sa* debates, *nagkakamali ako.*

How do the other girls take to you?
The first year was terrible because the girls did not know me. The seniors would bully us. I would answer them back, *minsan napapaaway na ako.* But you show your character, *tapos barkada ka na.* I get no special treatment; in fact, I always have to prove I know something, like if I have a new teacher. I never take advantage of my friendship with the permanent teachers.

Somebody described you to me as a free spirit. Is that true?
Yes, I'm very independent in everything and very headstrong, that's why *madalas ang* conflict. But I'm very reasonable and if your reason is very logical, I give in. *Pero pag hindi ko talaga kaya ang ni-reason sa akin, ay, imposible.*

As an only child, I learned that I have to do things on my own most of the time. Of course, I need people *pero kahit wala sila magagawa ko.* You cannot put me down. *Madadapa ako* but I always stand up. I crawl back. *Sabi nga ni Jay minsan para daw akong munggo, kahit saan ako itapon, tutubo. Sabi niya kahit mamatay siya* he won't worry about me and the children because *para akong munggo, magsu-*survive *kahit saan.*

How do you feel about compliments paid to your beauty?
Nakakasawa nang pakinggan. Okey lang. I know I look good, but looks to me are not important. A person should also be nice and kind. Like my boyfriends before, I would be teased, and *pangit-pangit naman,* like that. *Ang ganda-ganda ko raw, pero...Sabi ko hindi ako tumitingin sa hitsura ng tao.* What is important to me is the character of the person — is he nice, thoughtful, intelligent and a romantic like me, which you hardly find nowadays. I love romance. Take the romance out of my life and I'll die. It's so difficult for me to look for a guy *na makakatapat ako.* I like dinner by candlelight, nice music, nice setting, and you talk about a lot of things. I swoon over romantic novels, like *Gone with the Wind* and *Wuthering Heights.*

Have you had a lot of boyfriends?
After Jay, I had only about four, and they lasted a long time, about one or two years. *Pag medyo alanganin na,* I cut off the relationship right away.

What is the status of your relationship with Jay Ilagan?
Wala pang definite path. As of now, because of my daughter and because we decided we would try again — we were separated for a long time — this is a time to see if we are really meant for each other. But there's nothing definite. We're both very independent. *Parang* tryout stage. It's mainly the attitude — I'm very mature, *siya hindi pa masyado.* There are some things na *ginagawa ko, hindi niya maintindihan. Mas mabilis ang* growth *ko. Iba ang* line of thinking *niya.* And I go to school — that's one thing also. I tell him we have to keep on growing, we shouldn't stop, and school helps. So we'll see *kung ano ang mangyayari.* It's not just the fact that my daughter is there. Of course, we think about her. But we don't want a family that stays together *pero away nang* away. I cannot hide it when I'm really mad. And I'm not the *martir* type. Jay was my first love. I've been in love with him since I was 12. When I saw him I told myself *ito ang pakakasalan ko.* And I did marry him when I was 16. *Parang* love at first sight.

What was it in him that appealed to you?
He's very kind, very nice, thoughtful. He doesn't have a mean bone in him. But he's my opposite — he's not romantic. *Mabait na tao.* There's no competition between us, maybe just instances of jealousy. We're both possessive.

Did you try to hide the fact of your pregnancy from the movie press?
No, and then they said *nagtago ako.* I was everywhere — in Unimart, Rustan's, buying all my things — and I was so big. How can they say *nagtatago ako?* But I refused to give interviews, to have pictures taken. I even went to school. First semester, summer, I was in school. *Sabi ko,* why talk about it, why use it? That's one thing I don't want to do with my daughter — I don't want to use her. When I gave birth, *may mga* reporters *na pumunta* and I really

hated the idea because that was an intrusion on my privacy. *Sabi ko* it was all right to mention that I gave birth, but to take pictures and to go there! As much as possible, I want to keep my daughter away from the movies. I don't want to use her as a gimmick.

How are you raising your children?
In a way, I am strict with them. That's part of the training. When they're young, you mold them. They have to be trained, or else *wala. Ako lagi ang* enemy. Their *Lola* will say, "O *sige, iha,* you can get." Or their Papa, will say, "Okay, you can watch television." *Pag dumating ako,* O, why are you still awake? *Akyat na. Siyempre pag pinabayaan mo...* But I teach them to be independent, to think for themselves, what they really want to do. Like when we go shopping — what clothes do they want to wear. Ideas — I give them choices — what do they want to do. Do they want to play piano, or study dancing? *Kung saan nila gusto.* And I want their ideas to come out. But for certain things, like sleeping hours, I have rules. I can spend a whole afternoon talking to them and finding out how they feel and how their minds work so I get to know them better. Fantastic.

You have very sensible ideas for a young mother.
Kailangan. Children are changing nowadays. You cannot treat them the way I was trained before. No, I don't read books on child-raising, but I was brought up in a very strict way. It was not good, *hirap na hirap ako.* I'm not saying I don't control them at all, especially when their elders are talking. They can voice their opinions *kahit may matanda.* The little boy stays with my mother-in-law. The little girls are with me — they both go to Maryknoll, one is in kindergarten, the other in nursery. The boy goes to a Montessori school run by nuns — he's the same age as one of my girls. He's also in nursery. *Medyo pilyo, so sabi ko, maigi na doon. Sobra iyan.* They have love letters and phone calls.

Celebrity
October 15, 1979

Hilda Koronel turned 40 in January 1998. She had gone into a long retirement and full-time parenting, reemerging in 1996 as a principal figure in a controversy that gave her more media coverage than her return to the screen. She had accused her fourth husband, a doctor, of philandering; the case ended up in court. Since resuming her acting career, she has done three movies but mostly telesines (movies for TV). She has told movie reporters that she is happy enough being a full-time mother (to five children) and grandmother (by her adopted daughter Ivy). Jay Ilagan died in a motorcycle accident in the late Eighties, but by then he and Hilda had been separated and were with new partners. Asked by Philippine Star *entertainment writer Ricky Lo why her marriages always seemed to go wrong, she said, "Some (of my husbands) are weak, some are too tyrannical. They want to control me. I think some of them fell in love with Hilda Koronel the actress and not Susan Reid the person. Except Jay,* dahil artista din siya." *She harbored no bitterness in her heart, she said, and assured all who cared to know that "looking good and beautiful is the best revenge."*

Kuh Ledesma
Singing Is My Life, It's Me

Kuh Ledesma, by her own admission, is not an easy person to get along with, maybe even to live with. She has in fact been described more than once as aloof and snobbish. She is neither of these. She is only a very private person in the very public world of show business. Early this year, when she made public her impending motherhood, not a few thought her openness about her condition quite out of character, but she lent it her usual classy style by choosing to make the announcement during a series of concerts at one of Makati's plush music rooms.

Motherhood, however, which came to Kuh on Easter Sunday two months ago, is not the latest news about her. Next weekend she will be back at what she does best — singing — in two concerts at the Folk Arts Theater that will once again focus, as her concerts last year did, on the Filipino woman as superb musical artist. A fortnight ago, the very private singer opened the doors of her lovely San Juan home to Panorama *and allowed us glimpses into her personal life as well as the present and future directions of her career. Here then is Kuh, as far as she will allow us to see her.*

I was six and a half months pregnant when I made the announcement at Tavern on the Square. I had three concerts there on a Friday and a Saturday, then a repeat on a Wednesday, or was it a Tuesday? Anyway, I was wearing a big dress so my stomach didn't show. And I never told anyone except a friend of mine although my mother knew because as soon as I knew I was pregnant I called her up. Nobody else knew and nobody suspected anything.

On Friday night, after I told my audience, the people were very quiet. Later, after the show, I found out that they were saying, *Ano iyong sinabi ni Kuh? Totoo ba iyan? Baka nagbibiro lang, baka* gimmick *na naman iyan.* On the second day, some of them must

Kuh Ledesma

have heard the news already. I was cracking a few jokes and they laughed. *Nauna na ako* so they took it very well. Later, some people were saying, *Hindi naman iyan prinsesa, bakit ninyo pinagkakaguluhan iyan?*

The reason I kept the fact of my pregnancy secret for so long was I had ambivalent feelings about it, in terms of my fans also. I felt that I didn't want the children to think that I was doing the right thing. I knew that many people don't believe it should be done, I mean have a child out of wedlock. It's something that I can take, it's something that doesn't bother me, but it bothers me to think that the young kids who idolize me might follow in my footsteps. It bothers me up to this point; I don't want them to think that it's right. I mean, when they grow up and they think that it's right, they can take it, they can take what people will say about it, and they can live without feeling that they're a different part of society. In that sense I didn't think that I should be open about it or be proud of it. I just feel that this is my life. I also didn't want to keep my pregnancy for the rest of my life, at least not for my kid. It was a risk. I told myself this was a chance for me to find out if my fans would understand. They have to understand me as a person. They don't have to take everything that I do and do it, too.

I did want to have a baby. I didn't have anybody for a long time with whom I wanted to have a baby. But I said I'm not growing any younger and I'd like to have a baby before I turn 30. And it happened. I was supposed to have an operation to correct a condition called endometriosis. I couldn't have a baby. The doctor said I had to take the pill or I had to have an operation if I wanted to have a baby. But, to tell you the truth, I prayed hard, I said I don't want to have any operation. I'm scared of that.

When Isabella grows up, when the time comes, she'll understand. As long as she sees her father and her mother love each other, that should explain everything. At this point we do want to get married, but there are personal reasons I cannot share... Maybe a little more time...

I really don't believe in getting married young because a person changes and it takes a long time before you realize who the person you want to live with for the rest of your life is. I think when you go into something like marriage you shouldn't have any doubt in your mind. Sometimes also you think that this is the man, but when you live with him you realize there are things you don't know. I think it takes living with a person before you find out what he is all about. I'm not saying you have to know the person completely, but at least some things you'd like to see in him. There are things in a person that you don't want to know for the rest of your life, that he probably doesn't want you to know, too. It's a matter of respect. You don't want to show your *kaluluwa* even to the person you love because you want to keep a bit of mystery, to keep the interest going.

I tell my friends I can't describe the feeling of having a child of my own. I particularly like children but it's different when they're yours, you really want to hold them. Motherhood is making me more inspired. As much as possible, I take time even once a day to feed my baby and hold her. That's not very difficult because I do most of my work in the house. I even rehearse here.

A LOT OF PEOPLE say I'm an overnight success. That's not true. The people who just see you on TV and in concerts and hear you on the radio see only the success but don't see the pain that went with your experiences before that. In fact, I thought it took me a long time. I don't believe it was an easy time because even the other singers now did not go through what I had to — a year with a band, a year with the Music and Magic when we did four shows a night four times a week. Now you sing once a week and people write about you already. *Araw-araw kanta kami nang kanta* before they gave us our first concert. *Ngayon,* through media, you can actually build up anyone. The process is easier now.

I wonder whether the other artists put as much of their time (into their work) as I do into what I do. Every day I know exactly what I will do. All my waking moments are spent thinking of what I will do tomorrow. Even when I'm asleep, I am thinking this is what I should do, maybe this is better. When I'm on vacation I plan my career in terms of a year, in terms of six months, in terms of records. I think it's up to the person. I've always been like this, even when I was a child. When I found out what I really wanted to do, which was to sing, I said I'd work like crazy, I'd do all I could do so that this thing would not get out of my hands. When what you really want to do is there, all you have to do is work hard, put heart and soul into it to make it work. I think only the artist who works as much will make it. I can see it in Martin Nievera and Gary Valenciano — when I talk to them I can feel it. I was like that and I still am. I have not changed.

People say, strike hard when it's your time, just take all the things that come in *kasi mawawala ka rin naman*. That's not true. It's how you plan everything and how confident you feel you can go on. There are new ideas, so many things you can explore in music.

I would never have found out what I really wanted to do if I had not gone into it. It was an accident. Singing was always a part of my life, but if I hadn't auditioned because of a letter sent to me by Jet Montelibano of the Ensalada band, then I would never have found out *na, aba, pwede palang maging buhay ko talaga itong* music. Jet used to play the piano for me when I sang at programs at the University of San Agustin in Bacolod. He was studying engineering, I was taking up nursing. I didn't look for a job after college, but when I got Jet's letter I came to Manila to audition. And I became part of Ensalada.

When I was very young I was very shy. But I had to fight my shyness. When I joined Ensalada I told myself I wasn't going to be wishy-washy, I was going to sing. I told myself that once and for all, if I wanted this, I had to do it right. *May tawag kami noon, tugtog-pera. Araw-araw kasi.* We got paid P200 a day, singing the same songs, *walang* meaning, *walang* feeling. I told myself I didn't want to rot in a band and be a back-up girl all my life. I wanted to do solo. So when another band, the Rebirth Corporation, offered me a solo job, I joined them. I sang a lot of discos. *Ayaw ko naman ng* disco *kasi kanta ka nang kanta ng* disco *sila naman sayaw nang sayaw, hindi nakikinig. Ayaw ko na yata nito, sabi ko.* So I suggested to my friend Sandra Chavez, who became my manager, that we form a band. It was supposed to be Jet and me and five other guys. We auditioned at Regent but they wanted a show band and more girls. So we got three back-up girls. It must have taken me about three months before I could go onstage without feeling nervous. If you listen to our tapes, *talagang nanginginig ang mga boses.* You can stop there *kung natatakot ka,* but we had to go on.

The young female singers now are all so good. They each have their own style and character, they're all different from one another. I hope that I have helped set an example to these younger singers. It's good to be able to contribute something towards better entertainment, *hindi yung* you just appear on TV and sing a song, wear whatever you want. That's being disrespectful to entertainment and to people and to yourself. It's up to you — if you respect yoursef, you dress well, you sing well, you prepare for your number, then people will respect you. What you put in is what you get back.

A LOT OF PEOPLE tell me, why don't you go international? My not wanting to do that is probably mistaken for lack of confidence on my part. It's not that. If I decide to go international, I want to be sure that the people will back me all the way. It takes a lot of money and there are not very many people involved in the international recording business who would put a lot of money on an Asian girl. I'm not being pessimistic, but really, nothing of the sort has happened.

I think I want to stay right here in the Philippines. I feel there are so many things I want to do here, not only in terms of making records or doing concerts, but in terms of helping out some institutions through my concerts. There's a long-range plan I'm studying right now, but I can't go into detail yet. Let's just say that you can look at your career as a long-term thing because it's for something, not just singing. Okay, you make money, the producers make money, the people go back to your concerts, but what is it? It's still empty. But if there's a project that you do concerts for, our singing becomes worthwhile, it has more meaning and you'd like to go on, you feel more inspired. And you don't even stop with that project.

Another thing I'm interested in going into is movie production. It's capital intensive but it's something I'd like to do five years from now, perhaps work with a director to find out how a movie is made. I'd like to learn something else. For instance, when I started singing I didn't know anything about producing shows. But now I do. It's a matter of experiencing and learning.

Of course, I still see myself singing five years from now, for the rest of my life, in fact, even if just for a couple of friends. Singing is my life, it's really me. I sing at home all the time. My taste in music depends on my moods. Sometimes I want to go pop, sometimes classical, sometimes jazz. I like all kinds of music except hard rock. But there are particular songs that I like to sing; right. now it's George Benson's "In Your Eyes." Sometimes you just listen to a song and it goes over and over in your mind and even when you're about to sleep you can't because you still hear it.

I plan to raise Isabella with a lot of music, too. And a lot of love. It's nice to feel like a mother.

I really work hard at what I do and now I have someone to share it with. Like, I want to buy myself a farm where I can go every weekend. My parents never had a farm when I was a child. Thinking of a child on a farm gives me a good feeling. It's the same as seeing a child grow up — you see yourself.

Philippine Panorama
June 24, 1984

Kuh Ledesma has been commuting between the United States and Manila in pursuit of an international music career. On her eighteenth year as an entertainer, she finally realized her dream of launching an album in the U.S.. Her Music Museum in Greenhills, a popular venue for pop concerts, is 10 years old and going strong. Isabella, who showed an interest in an entertainment career even as a child, sings and is a regular on Viva-GMA-7's teen program T.G.I.S.. In December 1998 mother and daughter starred in a Christmas concert at the Music Museum. The Ice Queen's marriage to Louie Gonzalez has been the subject of rumor and speculation. She has told entertainment reporters that she has turned to God and the Bible for strength and solace.

LUISA LINSANGAN
The Women's Woman

Every week for more than 20 years now, except for an imposed hiatus in late 1972, Luisa H.A. Linsangan has been telling Filipino women from Aparri to Zamboanga how to whip up a perfect soufflé, how to tell if their men will love them forever, how to replenish their wardrobe the Parisian way, how to get the most out of a kiss, how to, in short, live happily ever after.

And every week the gospel according to Luisa H.A. Linsangan reaches at least a hundred thousand women, surely more if one counts, for example, the hundreds of women who skim through issues of *Women's Journal* while they wait for their turn at the beauty parlor or at their gynecologist's office.

A male friend tells me of a lady who lives by *Women's Journal*'s admonitions, measuring her husband by the yardstick prescribed by *WJ*, berating him each time she feels shortchanged by her choice of a mate. I am sure the lady is not unique.

I am sure that lady is, in fact, in the words of its editor, one of *WJ*'s "loyal, steady, faithful readers." These same readers earlier made the *Weekly Women's Magazine* the phenomenal publication that it was in terms of circulation. And they have made Ms. Linsangan the highest paid female journalist in the country today.

I am not, I am sorry to say, one of those hundred thousand and more Filipino women. I've never sworn by women's magazines, never needed them to tell me the kind of person — or woman — I should be. My hair stands on end when I read fashion text that runs like this: "Home is sweet, but the outside world beckons, and it's still a man's world. And it's still a woman's place to give him pleasure, to delight his discerning, critical eyes." Or this: "Please your man when he's had a bad day at the office; please him at

Luisa Linsangan

work, and at play, and during the long and short moments of the day that you spend with him."

But because she is a lady, Ms. Linsangan does not mind my not being a fan of *Women's Journal,* or of any other women's magazine for that matter. She tells me I am not a typical Filipina. Neither is she, she assures me. So what is a highly intelligent and articulate woman doing behind a magazine like *Women's Journal*?

"Do you believe in fate?" she asks me as I sit in her bare-walled office one afternoon. She is a fragile-looking woman whose most attractive features are her hands, which are long and graceful. Her voice is thin and small and she seems almost shy, nervous even, as she endlessly plays with one paper clip after another, deftly forming them into triangles as she speaks.

"Everything that has happened to me has been an accident," she says, answering her own question. She was enrolled in chemical engineering at the University of the Philippines when the war broke out. Even after the war she could not go back to school immediately because all the apparatus of the engineering department had been destroyed. It would be a two-year wait, too long for the young woman who had really wanted to become a journalist but whose father, a military man, did not want his daughter running around all day. Chemical engineering was a natural second choice. She excelled in math and science and her dream, when she finally got to U.P., was to be able to improve the leather industry in the country because she had always loved shoes and leather.

If not for fate, the country would have lost Luisa Linsangan to some middle-aged lady who, in the late Forties, had advertised for a traveling companion who could speak English and Spanish. Ms. Linsangan applied for the job but did not send in her application early enough. Instead, she landed a position in the advertising department of the *Evening Herald,* figuring that once she got into a newspaper, she could eventually find her way to the editorial department. She lasted a month in advertising but moved on to the *Star Reporter* and became a movie columnist. She had earlier turned down an offer to be the *Reporter's* society editor because "I am not the sort who cares who gives birth to whom, who married whom."

In 1950 the *Manila Times* launched a magazine for women called the *Weekly Women's Magazine.* Luisa Linsangan became a regular contributor to it, writing such stuff as who is the hunter and who is the hunted between men and women. She knew that kind of magazine writing well. A great deal of her education had come from *Glamour, Mademoiselle, Redbook, Harper's Bazaar* and *Cosmopolitan,* to all of which her mother subscribed. When Telly Albert Zulueta resigned the editorship of *Weekly Women's* in 1956, Ms. Linsangan was already not just a staff member but its associate editor.

The Roceses, however, were not too happy about the poor public response to the magazine and felt that perhaps the Filipina was not ready for it. Ms. Linsangan begged to disagree and asked to be allowed to experiment with the magazine for six months. Her chemical engineering background had taught her to analyze. "You do something, you give it at least six months before you decide whether it will click or not. I used the hit-and-miss method and waited for six months. I never made more than two changes at the same time. That way, I knew what was getting results." For instance, she had to drop the local fiction the magazine had been running because she found it caused circulation to drop.

In 1951, a year after the *Weekly Women's Magazine* was launched, circulation was 10,000. By 1955, it had risen to only 19,000. When Ms. Linsangan took over, she brought the figure up to 35,000 and by 1957, it was 55,000. When *Women's* closed shop with the imposition of martial law, it was lording it over all other magazines. "The success of *Women's,*" says Ms. Linsangan, "is the only thing that is not an accident to me." She is talking not only of *Women's Magazine* but also of *Women's Journal.*

She has always known the kind of magazine she wants.

"There must be a pretension to elegance, if not true elegance. It must have snob appeal. One secret of editing for women is you have to flatter them. So if a woman doesn't eat by candlelight and you know it, you don't let her know that you know it and you make her feel that you think she eats by candlelight. In other words, I don't insult my reader; I flatter her. She thinks I think this is how she lives. I want a magazine for the woman who is not going to copy what Nora Aunor is wearing but what Jackie Onassis is wearing. Then I would expect her to buy Amorsolos or Manansalas, maybe as investments or to decorate her home. I would give her Mills and Boon, together with all the class. Believe it or not, Mills and Boon is what our women understand. Even women in Forbes Park read Mills and Boon. But I would never, never try to ram literature down her throat."

When it comes to stories on sex, says Ms. Linsangan who denies she is a prude, "I have been told that we are still the most conservative." Much of the stuff of which *WJ* is made is escapist and its editor has a simple explanation for it: "I think a little sugarcoating won't hurt anybody. There is already a lot of bitterness. I believe in sugar-coated pills." And so life in the raw has no place in *WJ* — street urchins in Tondo, male cockfight spectators dressed in *kamiseta*, you know the kind of Philippine scenes we don't want tourists to see.

Ms. Linsangan is understandably peeved when other magazines for women come up and try to grab a share of her market. You would be, too, if you worked as hard as she does. On the day *WJ* hits the streets, its editor takes a bus from one terminal to the next just to see for herself which part of her magazine people read first. Or she takes a seat in a small Quiapo restaurant to find out what students look for in *Women's Journal*. In years past she recalls having spent a whole day at Alemar's just to watch the people who came in to buy Mills and Boon. That's how she knows for certain that even women in Forbes read mushy romances.

"The average woman," she says, "will not admit during surveys to reading sex stories first, but that's the truth." Astrology, however, is also high on the list of women's favorite reading; Ms. Linsangan says astrological articles pull up magazine sales to 130,000.

When that happens, she feels she can start putting in more of what she thinks women should get rather than what they want to get, such as more sober articles. But what happens? Circulation drops. What to do? "You have to compromise. You have to make money. I'm not that materialistic; I've never quoted a fee in all my life. But the idea is to give the reader what she wants, up to a limit. Like she might want Nora Aunor, but that would spoil the magazine, business-wise."

There is more, much more, to Luisa H.A. Linsangan than she cares to commit to paper. Her story should make a runaway best-seller someday, should she ever decide to write it. But she says she does not want to because it would hurt a lot of people. Her icy facade and her style of running the magazine ("an absolute dictatorship — it can't be any other way") notwithstanding, she is a nice, pleasant woman who just wants to make her publisher and her hundred thousand and more readers happy. Would that their definition of happiness did not have to exclude intelligence.

Celebrity
September 15, 1979

Luisa H. Linsangan retired from the Journal group of publications in 1986 and set up her own magazine which she called **Marie Claire.** *Her editorial touch, however, did not work its magic on the new publication and the magazine folded up after only a few years. In the summer of 1996 Ms. Linsangan died of cardiac arrest brought on by complications from an asthma attack.*

Lisa Macuja
On Her Way Up

The young dancer is home, but not for long, just long enough to relish all that she missed during the two years she was attending ballet school in faraway Leningrad.

Lisa Macuja, all of 19 but remarkably poised and self-confident, frets about the limbering up she has not been doing enough of since coming home. A dancer never rests, never allows her muscles to relax, not even while she is on vacation, she says. Already, she has added two kilos to her dancing weight of 43; she is feeling heavy. In Russia she had grown accustomed to doing practice exercises at one in the afternoon. Since she arrived in early July, her body has had to readjust to a much later schedule, as well as to the warm weather, which is hot compared even to summer in Leningrad.

But she is happy to be home and to be bearing good tidings to her countrymen: after only two years of rigorous ballet training in Leningrad, she will be, when she returns there this month, the very first non-Russian member of the Kirov Ballet. She has been invited to join the ranks of the famous company which has produced over the decades such demigods as Pavlova, Nijinski, Ulanova, Sergeyev, Dudinskaya, Makarova, Baryshnikov and Nureyev. With such an exceptional feat by a young Filipino, the seeming irrelevance of ballet to the current political and economic turmoil could be forgiven.

Lisa's feat was no miracle. It was achieved at no little cost to a young girl who gave up a sheltered, comfortably bourgeois life for the spartan discipline, harsh climate and totally alien communist lifestyle of Russia. She could have gone to London, for she had also been accepted into the Royal Academy of Dancing, and felt more instantly at home. Instead she took the road no Filipino

LISA MACUJA

before her had taken and in doing so, made her success so much sweeter. Those who know Lisa well are not surprised; they say they have never known her to shirk from a challenge.

Yet she had been unusually shy as a child. When she took the entrance examinations for prep at St. Theresa's College in Quezon City, she was so bashful she flunked her interview. The nuns took her in only because she did very well in the written tests. As she found her metier in school, however, she gained confidence in herself, in the process becoming talkative, energetic, *magulo*. Her mother knew she was ripe for ballet classes.

Susan Pacheco Macuja, a vivacious woman in her early forties, had nurtured dreams of becoming a ballerina in her youth. But she grew up during the era of ultraconservatism in the Catholic Church, when even classical ballet was condemned as obscene and eventually banned from the cultural scene. So ended, after five blissful years of ballet, Susan's dream of a dancing career.

When Lisa was nine she was enrolled in Felicitas Radaic's School of Dance (later renamed Dance Theater Philippines) which even then was housed at St. Theresa's. It was a convenient arrangement for Lisa, who soon came to consider ballet class as part of her routine twice a week, an hour each time. Ballet to her was a hobby, nothing more. In the meantime Susan Macuja encouraged her daughter's dancing and, being a true balletomane, would take her along to every ballet concert at the Cultural Center. Lisa would sleep through most of the performances, but one evening she sat up and watched and was enchanted. The dancer onstage was Margot Fonteyn. At a school recital two years later, Lisa was assigned to dance the Bluebird pas de deux. For the first time she danced with enthusiasm. After that, she relates, "I got to love ballet, really like it."

When she saw visiting superstars Yoko Morishita and Fernando Bujones in *Swan Lake* at the CCP, she was hooked. She knew what she wanted in life. Morishita is Asian and short, the teenager told herself, yet she made it to the top. "I loved her performance so much that I wanted to be a ballerina also. There was that goal and I would work at it."

The way to that goal was not to be smooth and clear, however. When Lisa was 15 she fractured her left ankle during a rehearsal.

She was grounded for four months while the fractured leg healed and then while she underwent therapy. "It was terrible. I thought maybe it was useless to continue. Maybe the Lord had different plans for me and I was not really meant to dance." She would test herself, she resolved, the way she has tested herself many times since.

The year-end examinations given by England's Royal Academy of Dancing to dancers of Dance Theater Philippines were approaching. That, Lisa thought, would be a good time to see what the future had in store for her. If she received a rating of either honors or "highly commended," the two highest possible marks, she would go on. If, on the other hand, her grade was anything lower, she would quit, perhaps be the accountant her father and her paternal grandmother were still hoping she would be. As things turned out, she got a rating of "highly commended."

She was then in her last year of high school, a tough time for any student, but tougher still for someone who had to strike a balance between her studies and her dancing. It was a time of unbelievable pressure, physical and mental, for her. At the peak of the Dance Theater Philippines season she would have rehearsals every night until 10, then she would go home and study for next day's classes, sleep at two or four in the morning, and be up for school at six. Her parents suggested she quit ballet temporarily, at least till after graduation. She refused. At the St. Theresa's commencement exercises that year, Lisa was class salutatorian.

At Dance Theater Philippines she had risen to become principal soloist and was already being noticed for her exceptional virtuosity. Ballets were specially choreographed for her by Basilio Esteban Villaruz and Michael Hennessy. There was no question in her mind that after high school she would skip college in favor of further studies in ballet. She wrote the Royal Academy of Dancing and, on the basis of her "highly commended" certificate, was accepted for a two-year course. Her instincts told her, however, that something even better might come along.

A few months before her graduation, her father Cesar, who was then head of the Philippine International Trading Corporation, was entertaining a trade delegation from Moscow. One night he took his guests to a performance of Dance Theater, where Lisa was dancing. He casually mentioned to the Russians that his daughter wanted more than anything else to undergo further training in ballet and had heard much about the ballet schools in Russia. Then and there, after watching Lisa onstage, the delegation offered to inquire about a scholarship for her when they returned home. So when classes started at the Royal Academy Lisa was still here, pinning her hopes on Leningrad. She was willing to wait. And she was not disappointed. By October 1982 she and fellow Dance Theater soloist Mary Anne Santamaria were on a plane bound for Moscow, and from there, Leningrad. Lisa was only 17.

"I wanted to see and experience for myself how it is to live in Russia, in a communist country," she says to explain why she chose Leningrad, besides the very obvious reason that it has the world's oldest ballet academy. By an uncanny twist of fate, she had done a term paper on Russian literature in her senior year and, in the course of researching on Russia's history and its writers, had become fascinated by the country. Little did she know that she would actually go there.

Lisa and Mary Anne became the very first Filipino scholars of the legendary Vaganova Choreographic Institute, whose professional ballet company is the famous Kirov. The school does not accept students from capitalist countries but opens its doors to those from the socialist states, the developing world and Eastern Europe. While other Asians had enrolled there in the past, the two young Filipino women found themselves the only representatives of their part of the world in 1982.

Lisa had never before been away from her family. Nor was the separation any easier on the Macujas. "Nobody we knew had ever seen Russia," says Susan, "and it was so far away." But neither she nor her husband ever tried to dissuade their eldest child from going. They knew her well enough to realize that when she set her heart on a goal she would pursue it to the end.

Lisa had led an incredibly sheltered life. Until senior high she was taken to school and back home by her mother. Only three times in her life had she gone anywhere by public transport and in all those instances she was always with one of her family's trusted helpers. But, insists her mother, she was not spoiled, and that makes a lot of difference.

Adjusting to life in Leningrad involved a 180-degree turn for Lisa. Back home she had her own prettily furnished bedroom and bathroom and now she was to share one toilet and one bathtub with 15 other students in her dormitory. She would wash her own clothes, cook her own food. And she would begin a punishing regimen of classes, rehearsals, more classes, more rehearsals.

On their first day in Leningrad she and Mary Anne were aghast to discover that absolutely no one spoke English. Happily, they both began Russian language lessons that very day. Lisa did so well that after a month she could grasp the fundamentals of the language and in two more months was speaking it and even reading Russian literature. At the end of the language course she received a grade of 6, the highest possible rating.

Of course, she was homesick. She was miserable the first two weeks, and she would call up her parents and tearfully beg them to pray over her. When she came home for Christmas she refused to go back. Only her parents' insistence made her return to Leningrad. Once settled there, she wrote her parents that she was glad she had taken their advice.

"After the first six months there I was used to it already," Lisa says. "I wasn't really thinking of what I was missing out on. I was thinking instead of what I was gaining in Leningrad, and that made quite a difference, especially when I would think about the ballet part, what I was learning, the roles I was rehearsing and dancing. These were things that would not be possible back home."

In Russia classical ballet dancers undergo eight to 10 years of study and training. The Vaganova Choreographic Institute has an eight-year course for students from the age of 10. Although Lisa was qualified for the eighth and final grade, she decided to start from the seventh since she would be there for two years. Aside from her dance subjects — character dancing, classic duet dance, actress skill, historico-genre dance — and the language course, she also took Russian history.

All students at the Institute are scholars who receive a monthly stipend of 100 ruble (US$120). Everything, including pointe shoes, is provided free, except food which must be bought with the stipend. Food in Russia, says Lisa, is cheap and plentiful, but there is little variety. Before Lisa left for Moscow, pianist and Russian scholar Rowena Arrieta had warned her to bring along some food provisions, but Lisa would not listen. She would get by on what was available, she said. Before long, however, she was pining for such capitalist staples as a Big Mac, Shakey's pizza and a good Chinese meal, all of which are unheard of in Russia.

When her mother planned her first visit to Leningrad, Lisa had a long list of *bilin* for her. The musts included *siopao,* which were stored for a week in the Macuja freezer before being packed in towels for the long trip; *turrones de casuy, pastillas de leche,* Tang orange juice, pineapple juice, mayonnaise, tuna spread, sandwich spread, Nescafe coffee, *patis,* vinegar, Spam, pork and beans, as well as sanitary napkins (unavailable in the Soviet Union) and gift-wrapping paper.

"*Kawawa talaga yan,*" Susan moans, "*nahirapan.*" She should know. On three visits to Leningrad these past two years, Susan Macuja lived with her daughter in the dorm and saw for herself the spartan lifestyle for which Lisa had traded in her comfortable life in Manila. But Lisa hardly speaks of the hardships and the strain unless one asks her. "It was hard work, emotionally, mentally and physically," says Susan. There was one big factor, though, that made a lot of difference. Lisa did not mind the difficulties because she loved what she was doing and was happy doing it. She was dedicated to her art and the challenge she was given, and she was willing to pay for it.

Classes in Leningrad started at one in the afternoon with practice and ended at 8:30 p.m. with rehearsals. By tradition, students of the school present in January each year the full-length version of Tchaikovsky's *Nutcracker.* On her first year Lisa was tapped to be one of the Snowflakes in the corps de ballet. It was a stage debut duly noted by Novosti Press Agency: "The slender, feather light, fragile-looking girl fascinated the audiences by her debut... last winter." Lisa could not believe the many curtain calls she had to take. The following school year, she was chosen to dance the lead role of Masha in *The Nutcracker.* The role is traditionally given to the student whom the school considers the ballerina of the moment. It was given for the first time to a foreigner, enough reason for Russian television to cover the event.

It was, Lisa told a reporter excitedly, "the happiest day of my life." In praising her performance, Konstantin Sergeyev, the artistic director of the Institute, described her as "artistically and musically gifted and very industrious."

Things moved at a fast clip from then on for Lisa. After her success as Masha, she performed the Harlequinade pas de deux for the March concerts at the Kirov Theater. "My partner did not know how else to bow because the audience just would not let us go." She modestly adds, however, that "a lot of the credit goes to my partner, a classmate, who was fantastic."

By April, she was ready for the state examinations in classical ballet given to all graduating classes at the school and attended by a 10-person jury that included big names in Russian ballet as well as officials from Moscow. Also there to observe were the artistic director of the Kirov and other students, teachers and company dancers.

"I was nervous," Lisa narrates, "because it was not a performance, it was a class, and it was not continuous dancing movement but exercises. So there were breaks, therefore time to get nervous. I tied the ribbons of my shoes so tight blood didn't flow. When the fifth exercise came I got the cramps suddenly in both calves. They hardened like rocks. My teacher saw that something was wrong. *Malaking* drama. The physiotherapist came and gave me a massage and they had to use scissors to cut the ribbons. I said I'd continue the exams. So I ended up doing one whole exercise all by myself."

One of the last exercises Lisa had to do was the 32 consecutive fouette turns on one leg without touching the floor with the other. It is considered a virtuoso feat, more so when done on painful calves. The artistic director of the Kirov approached Lisa's teacher and said she should not be made to do more; everything was clear, he added. When her teacher told Lisa to stop she refused. She completed the exam but collapsed once it was all over. When she regained consciousness the most exciting news awaited her. She had been invited by the Kirov's artistic director himself to join the company, with the promise that she would be given the opportunity to dance actively.

"I was really speechless, dumbstruck. My teacher had this big smile on her face and she asked me if I was satisfied and happy. I said yes, of course. Then I ran into the dressing room, crying." For the graduation program Lisa again was given the plum role of Kitri in *Don Quixote*. "The school authorities went as far as to try to stop us from dancing *Don Quixote* because they didn't want foreigners to look and dance better than the students from Leningrad itself," she says. Yet dance *Don Quixote* they did.

Susan Macuja was one of five Filipinos in the large audience (the others were Lisa's former teacher Basilio Esteban Villaruz, Mary Anne Santamaria's parents and Lisa's grandmother, who had by now become one of her most ardent fans) and she says she wept as her daughter took one curtain call after another. Susan was glad, in fact, that there were other Filipinos to witness the overwhelming audience reaction to her daughter's dancing: she did not want to be accused back home of exaggerating her account of that program.

By now, it was clear that Lisa had established a following among the Leningraders. Her dressing room was flooded with flowers from people in the audience. When she came out of the theater, looking unballerina-like in t-shirt and jeans and a jacket, a crowd was waiting to ask for her autograph and about her plans for the future. One old lady, upon being told that Lisa was joining the Kirov the following season, could not contain her joy. "Then all the flowers will be for Lisa," she told Susan. The newspapers were no less profuse in their praise. Glowed the *Leningradskaya Pravada:* "The Leningrad ballet school has educated a new Filipino prima ballerina notable for stability in the performance of most repertoire." The newspaper *Vecheray Leningrad* described Lisa's performance as "a superb achievement of classical ballet."

One need not be a balletomane to see that what must captivate Lisa Macuja's audience is her happy style of dancing — what Filipinos would call *"bigay na bigay."* There is no holding back with her, no tenseness, for all nervousness leaves her the moment she comes onstage. And even when she falls, as she once did in Leningrad, her poise and élan never leave her.

"It becomes a high when you're onstage dancing and you feel the audience enjoying your dancing," she explains. "That's why I don't like dancing something I don't feel comfortable with yet. I cannot enjoy myself if I still have to think. Some way or other the audience feels that you're having a hard time. People go to the theater to enjoy themselves, to forget. An artist has a responsibility to her audience to give much pleasure."

"I didn't dream of this," she sighs, referring to the contract with the Kirov. The theater director had wanted her to sign up for five years, or at least for three. Cesar Macuja would allow his daughter only a year. Yet she says that if she sees a future for herself in the company she may extend her stay to the maximum five-year period. It all depends, she says, on how her first season, which starts on August 23, will go. She realizes all too well that her being a foreigner may stand in the way of her full development in the company.

Had the Kirov not taken an interest in her she would have applied and auditioned for a position in either a European or an American company. She was never worried that she would have nowhere to go, not with a curriculum vitae that includes dancing, among other roles, Masha in *The Nutcracker*, and a certificate from the school that rated her "excellent" in four subjects — classic dance, classic-duet dance, actress skill and historico-genre dance — and "good" in character dance, and a grade of 5, the highest possible, in the state examinations. What about home? one asks. One sympathizes with her reply: "I just couldn't come back here. I would deteriorate here."

She does have plans for her country, however. But first she must fulfill her dream — of dancing certain roles as prima ballerina, like Kitri and Giselle and Odette/Odile and Raimonda. And then when she is 35 or 40 she will quit dancing and come home — "to teach ballet here the way it was taught to me in Leningrad." She would want to fill the need for a "very, very good school" that would supply companies with competent dancers, girls and boys who will enter school at the age of nine or 10 for the sole purpose of becoming professional ballet dancers.

Someday, too, she would want to marry and have a daughter who will, hopefully, follow in her mother's footsteps. There is, she admits coyly, a "special friend" back in Leningrad ("Don't you wonder why my Russian has improved?" she teases) but nothing very serious. A dancer has not much time for a social life; and Lisa, says her mother proudly, has never been crazy about phone calls or parties. It is specially true now that she is a dancer. "There's simply no energy left," she sighs.

There are those among Lisa's countrymen, even among ballet teachers, says her mother, who still don't believe that Lisa was taken in by the Kirov. "Did they think we would put out press releases *na* lies?" she asks indignantly.

The petty whispers of envious tongues do not bother Cesar Macuja one bit. He is one proud father these days, his daughter's Number One fan. "What I'm happy about," he beams, "is that both the Russians and the Filipinos admire her very much. And it is the kind of admiration that is for the total person — her attitudes, her relationships with people, and that makes me feel especially good."

That, after all, is what matters in the final analysis: the human factor. It was Margot Fonteyn who said in her autobiography, "Great artists are people who find the way to be themselves in their art. Any sort of pretension induces mediocrity in art and life alike."

Here then is to Lisa Macuja — and to the great artist and great person she could become.

Philippine Panorama
August 5, 1984

For the past four years, Lisa Macuja has been the associate artistic director and principal dancer of her own company, Ballet Manila, which is widening the audience for ballet through outreach programs. Her goal is to make Ballet Manila the strongest classical ballet company in the country. She married business tycoon, artist and art patron Fred Elizalde in a well-publicized wedding on June 7, 1997 and gave birth to their first child, Missy, on July 28, 1998.

Nonoy Straight Out of Marcelo

Nonoy Marcelo opens the door and his curious round eyes ask you to come in. He is wearing the Indian *kurta* again, the black one with white floral embroidery, which he prefers to tuck into his denim pants. The cotton shirt fails to hide an unattractive paunch. It's not a paunch, he protests, he simply has to walk around with his stomach thrown out to relieve a backache he acquired after having sat through three movies straight.

Tisoy's creator is home, more or less to stay. These days he is holed up in a small apartment in Ermita, in a building that has definitely seen better days. Everywhere in the apartment there is an air of transiency, of uncertainty. The anteroom is cluttered with old newspapers, and the bamboo cage that housed two *martinez* birds he bought from a vendor some weeks ago is gone from the old chair on which it sat when you last saw him. One of the birds has died; the other has been deposited with the caretaker of the building. In the tiny white kitchen the piece de resistance is Mr. Coffee, a sparkling new white coffeemaker, one of only two things Marcelo brought back from the States, besides his clothes. He likes his coffee black, no sugar, no cream, and he professes not to understand why other people must have sugar and cream in theirs.

The largest room in the apartment holds a battered refrigerator, a double bed, an artist's table, an easel, a desk, a couple of chairs, a few paintings. The fridge is completely in character with the apartment: it is old and deteriorating. It is also, Marcelo tells you, a paradise for cockroaches. (One evening, in fact, he got so annoyed with the pests he lined the inside of the fridge door with a long strip of tape to trap them dead. The scheme worked.)

A royal-blue quilted bedspread covers the bed, which really looks like it hasn't been slept on (Marcelo tells his mother he sleeps on the floor). The bedspread is the only other thing that

Nonoy Marcelo

looks Stateside, but you are too polite to ask whether it belongs to him or to his landlord.

Actually, the one other thing Marcelo packed for the trip home to Manila was his Sony stereo tape recorder, which you presently see in the half-opened clothes closet. There is more food in the room: a package of *pan de sal*, still hot when his mother's driver delivered it all the way from Malabon that morning, lies unopened on the table; and comfortably perched atop the faded lampshade is a crumpled paper bag that contains, Marcelo says, one *siopao*.

Marcelo is not much of an eater, nor too much of a talker, until he has warmed up to both you and the subject. His conversation is confusing, garbled, disorganized. You need both a photographic memory and utmost patience: the first to retain what he says and then to relate it to something he will say minutes from now, and the second to unscramble his syllables. Right now his conversation shifts from an amused recollection of his swimming lessons in the Carlos Moran Sison family pool in Forbes Park (a futile effort — the young man from Malabon never learned how to swim, even after, as one of his friends quipped, he had swallowed half of Prissy Sison's swimming pool) to his hippie buttons of the mid-Sixties which bore such Marcelo catchphrases as *Dyahe ang mahirap, Legalized OA, Born Tanga*. And then he stops abruptly, cocks one ear towards the stereo set in his closet, and excitedly says, "*Iyan lang ang hinihintay ko, e.*" His face is beaming. The music is Mozart's Bassoon Concerto and it is the bassoon solo he has been waiting for. Now he hums along with it. For a while, all seems well with his world.

NONOY MARCELO'S world has always been exciting, rather eccentric, very nonconformist, terribly colorful. It has been so by his own choice. Well, mostly. Like, you can't believe him when he tells you that for the first five years of his life he was raised as a girl. Not until, on your next visit with him, he proudly shows you a tiny picture album. There, in a family picture taken in Antipolo, is Nonoy as a little "girl," round-eyed and pretty in a checkered dress with lacy bib and a barrette in "her" hair. There are more pictures of Baby, as he was called, with his brothers or by himself, and they are of a baby girl, with shapely legs, his mother likes to remember. He did not know about this period in his life until much later when he saw those pictures and, not being sure which one he was, asked who the other little girl was. (Of the five Marcelo children, only the eldest, Emy, is a girl.)

Nonoy Marcelo was named after his maternal grandfather, a telegraph operator during the Philippine Revolution. He does not remember his father, a mechanical engineer who volunteered for action in the war and was killed by the Japanese on his very first day at the front. Gregorio Marcelo was dean of the Institute of Technology at Far Eastern University and one of the founders of National University. Nonoy, his third son, remembers a childhood in which, maternal protestations to the contrary, he felt that being the fourth child, and not a very attractive one at that, he did not have much of a chance in the *"pagandahan* contest" and in the competition for attention. *"Parang may* need," he says self-consciously. *"Ito hindi na* drama." He discovered that *"nakakakuha lang ako ng* attention *pag nagsisipag ako. Kaya nagsipag ako ng katakot-takot, sa lahat."*

He learned to draw even before he started school. An uncle, Jose Zabala Santos, who made illustrations for Pilipino *komik* strips such as Popoy and Lucas Malakas, lived on the second floor of the Marcelo home. Nonoy was his eager pupil. At one time Santos was doing work for *Halakhak Komiks* and Nonoy remembers that the very first word he learned to read, when he was in grade one, was the word *halakhak*.

Before long, he was doing his own comic strips and producing his own comic books, with guest cartoonists like Malang and Alcala, his uncle's colleagues. Not having too many toys to play with, he learned to invent his own, such as a whole town complete with skyscrapers, residential area, road system and people, which he and a brother built out of shoe boxes, grocery boxes and class cards his mother Rita, an English professor at FEU, had discarded. Emy Marcelo Pascual recalls that Nonoy also made an imaginary kingdom out of cardboard and, for the children in the neighborhood, cardboard picture shows with sound effects he himself produced, admission to which was with paper money he himself designed.

When he was about nine and in fourth grade, he became bothered by Darwin's theory of evolution, which somehow did not jibe with what the Maryknoll sisters at St. James Academy in Malabon were teaching him. The question of where he would go after death gave him sleepless nights and finally a feeling of weightlessness he couldn't explain.

A doctor prescribed complete rest for a year. Nonoy spent the time drawing. When he went back to school, it was with a vengeance. He landed in the honor roll, was class president until high school, became a figure to reckon with on campus. He was also the bully who once prohibited the rest of his class from raising their hands. About a month and a half before he was to graduate, a classmate got hold of a copy of the English test and circulated it. The news leaked to the sisters and everyone involved was suspended at first and later expelled. Nonoy was implicated. *"Ang ermat ko nag-Aling Otik,"* he says, *"pero* expelled *pa rin. Ako raw ang* mastermind." His record of wrongdoing and mischief, which had earlier earned him a stern warning from the nuns, worked against him this time. He couldn't have cheated in English, he says, for it was a subject in which he excelled. Maybe, he says in jest, if that had been a test paper in math...

And so the once and future high school graduate found himself, just a few weeks before graduation, without a school. He spent the rest of the school year at National Teachers College but, without Form 138 to show that he had graduated, he could not get into the University of the Philippines where he was hoping to take fine arts. His mother "smuggled" him, as he puts it, into FEU where, while waiting for his Form 138, he took as many subjects as he could but concentrated on political science. By the time he was through, he also had enough units in English and psychology to claim them as his other major areas.

At FEU he met Alejandro Roces, then dean of the Arts and Sciences Department. Says Roces today: "I could see that he was a sharp fellow. Many of the professors were complaining to me that all he did in class was draw. So I took a look at his drawings and realized that he had talent — he could draw exact likenesses of his professors." Anding Roces placed Nonoy Marcelo on the staff of the *Advocate* and the boy from Malabon created a sensation both inside and outside the campus with a comic strip on an eccentric campus character he called Ptyk.

Anding Roces had loftier dreams for Marcelo. At a board meeting of the *Manila Times,* Roces introduced Marcelo to his colleagues. The introductions over, he asked Nonoy to step out. A few minutes later, when Roces asked his young friend to come into the room again, Marcelo already had sketches to show of all the board members. He had done them while waiting to be summoned back to the board room. The *Times* executives were impressed, but not enough to give Marcelo what he wanted — a strip in the *Times. Times* publisher Joaquin P. "Chino" Roces introduced Marcelo to Aguilar "Abe" Cruz, editor of the *Times's* sister paper, *The Daily Mirror.* "Roces said I might be able to use him," Cruz recalls. "I was familiar with Nonoy's works in the *Advocate* and admired his talent." Marcelo started out doing "Plain Folks," a daily cartoon for the *Mirror.*

IT WAS NOT until he won the best three cartoon prizes in the annual competition of the Society of Philippine Illustrators and Cartoonists (SPIC) that year that the *Times* publisher agreed to give him space for his own strip. He had not expected Chino Roces's offer to come so soon.

Student life was the only thing he knew well, but he could not do Ptyk. Then Marcelo remembered a classmate of his, a good-looking mestizo who was rather stupid but popular with the girls. And so was born "Tisoy." The face of his new hero he modeled after artist and columnist Alfredo R. Roces, and around "Tisoy" Marcelo built a coterie of other characters — *Aling* Otik, Clip, Caligula, Maribubut, Pomposa, Gemmo, Tikyo, Professor Naspu — so real and believable they became instant hits with the public.

Anding Roces has a ready explanation for the spectacular success of "Tisoy." "The cartoons of Gat and Malang have always had a very basic defect — their people don't look like Filipinos. But Nonoy's people always have from the beginning. That is why I can identify the people in his drawings. '*Tisoy*' is still the first truly original Filipino cartoon. It draws materials from life."

In the mid-Sixties a study of "Tisoy" conducted by a graduate student of the U.P. Institute of Mass Communication showed 81 percent of the respondents, all students, rated it as the "best strip" and more readers preferred it to "Peanuts."

Marcelo's cartoons in the Sixties, says Roces, were "sociological commentaries." Bibsy Carballo, who worked with Marcelo at both the *Times* and the *Mirror*, says, "I liked his satirical style. It was very good because *nakukuha niya ang* lingo of the times. As far as I was concerned, he was our best cartoonist then."

By the late Sixties Marcelo was doing five cartoons daily: two editorial cartoons for the *Daily Star*, "Plain Folks" for the *Daily Mirror*, "Tisoy" for the *Sunday Times* and "Jack Parak." On Sundays he did "Tatang" for the *Sunday Times Magazine* and a longer "Tisoy" strip, both of them in color. "Tisoy" had also been adapted for television and producers bought the rights to film it, but no agreement could be reached as to the stars.

Marcelo produced hippie buttons and Christmas cards, and did op art paintings which were proudly exhibited at Indios Bravos, then the favorite haunt of bohemians, artists, counterculture freaks. He also published two books — *Plain Folks* and *Tisoy*. He had two MG sportscars and a driver, and he had his sights set on acquiring a Mercedes as well.

And then, as he puts it, the "love effect" hit him. It wasn't the first time, but this one hit him hard. One day in 1969 Marcelo picked up his brother at the latter's office and asked to be taken to the airport. "*Sabi ko papunta akong* Hong Kong, *ang mga* layout *naiwan sa* desk, *nakakalat.*" It was the longest coffee break he had ever taken. Take that to mean he never came back.

He left at 3, and by 4:30 was in Hong Kong, which he thought would be just a stopover. He wanted to go to New York because, besides the "love effect," he wanted to fulfill a cherished dream of producing an animated film. Once in Hong Kong he was able to land two jobs with the help of Filipino friends — doing a full-page cartoon every Sunday for the *South China Morning Post* and being an advertising artist at Chase Compton. A Mr. Chow, who owned Chase Compton, wanted all his men properly attired. For Marcelo that meant a suit and a haircut. He actually reported for work — and with his hair cut short. *"Ginawa ko alang-alang sa pag-ibig. Sa buong buhay ko noon lang ulit ako nag-shampoo. Nawala ang buhok ko. Nagmukhang plantsado."*

He eventually lost his job at Chase Compton because he was always late and he refused to get another haircut. Chow was reluctant to let him go, and at first agreed to allow Marcelo to work only half-day, then *"por piraso,"* but the routine had become too much for the young man who ached to be free.

On New Year's Eve he had to fly to the U.S. because his visa was due to expire. He headed for New York where he had friends and there found a job illustrating books. He did cartoons for *Sick* magazine or dabbled in printmaking and learned all he could about filmmaking and animation. In between he tried the commune life and found it to his liking, bought himself a house in Manhattan, got an apartment in Greenwich Village, and a red MG besides. He also became pretty adept at making stained-glass Tiffany lamps.

Nonoy Marcelo has not become Americanized, nor *burgis*. He can ape American English *"pero dyahe akong magsalita."* Says he: *"Wala akong* illusions about being *burgis. Ang mga taong* okay *sa akin iyong mga ilagay mo sa* deserted place *at i-*strip *mo ng lahat at tingnan mo kung paano sila magsu-*survive. *Ang sarili ko, bini-*brace *ko sa lahat, sa wala, sa* zero *parati. Sa gayon walang* envy, *wala kang hahanapin,* I can survive on the barest essentials."

When he finally decided to come home, after meeting artist Mauro Malang Santos in New York and being persuaded to come back and maybe work out arrangements for his dream animated film here, he took another long coffee break. While in Washington, D.C., he drove back to New York and got himself a plane ticket for Manila.

But before that, in November 1975, he had slipped into town quietly and stayed for a month. His sister Emy remembers that when he stepped out of the plane she almost howled. He looked so tidy and formal — he actually wore a suit, with a necktie yet, and clean shoes. He had thought that under Marcos's New Society his old unkempt self would no longer be acceptable. He had come for a look-see then. By October last year he was back, long hair and all, and with more definite plans.

The moment he saw the Metro Manila Aides at the airport he knew what he wanted to do with *Aling* Otik. Abe Cruz, his former boss at the *Mirror*, thinks Marcelo's cartoons "are much better now than before, more witty, more spontaneous." Yet there are those, like Bibsy Carballo, who believe "Tisoy" has "outlived itself," perhaps because "Tisoy" no longer stings, it can no longer engage in political satire.

BUT WHILE Marcelo's friends may disagree on "Tisoy"'s worth today, they are unanimous on one thing. Nonoy Marcelo, they say, has not changed. They love to recall his *Times* and *Mirror* days when he followed no rules, respected no conventions. Anding Roces, as head of the FEU Arts and Sciences Department and later as secretary of education, took Marcelo along on many trips of discovery and exploration — when the latter "discovered" the Ati-atihan and Moriones festivals, did research on the sarimanok, led a team to the Tabon Caves in Palawan. "I have a thousand stories to tell about Nonoy," says Roces.

"Once, when we were in Marinduque, a man approached me and tried to sell me a *musang* (wildcat). I refused and told him no one would buy a *musang*. Sometime later the same man came back and told me I had been wrong, someone had bought the animal. When I boarded the plane for home, there was Nonoy with a cage on his lap and the *musang* inside. When he got home the *musang* did not want to eat, so Nonoy went about his house shooting rats to feed his pet." That is not the only strange pet Nonoy has acquired from a trip. He once brought home a chameleon from Palawan.

"Another time," Roces continues, "we were on top of a mountain and Nonoy found a long branch, about 12 feet long, and very heavy. It fascinated him. I asked him what he wanted to do with it. He said he was taking it home because it was beautiful. He put it on his back, *pasang krus* style, climbed all the way down the mountain with it. When we got to our vehicle he realized he couldn't take the whole thing along, so he cut it up and brought just a piece home."

Roces tells about the time Marcelo planted rice on the roof of his house in Malabon. Marcelo corrects the story: he planted not only rice, he says, but also squash and *ampalaya*. He carted up some earth and set up a wooden enclosure around his "farm" without anyone in his family knowing what he was up to. He did not realize that all this time *"iyong lupa kinakain ang yero."* One day a typhoon hit town and water came through to the Marcelo kitchen from the ceiling. Mrs. Marcelo had the shock of her life, and an even greater shock when she discovered how that happened.

Of their *Times-Mirror* days, Bibsy Carballo says, "He even brought his *baon* to the office, K-rations which he bought at PX stores, sometimes in Angeles. Everything was in his desk — *nabubulok na saging, balut, damit,* etc. And he hated it when someone cleaned up his desk. When he made phone calls he would hide under his desk — *parang daga,* as the people in the office described him."

Carballo recalls that on a visit to the Marcelo home in Malabon she saw a wooden casket. It was where Marcelo slept, *"kung minsan lang naman,"* he clarifies. When he slept in the *Times* office, Anding Roces says, "He would sit in his swivel chair, lean back, cover his face with a handkerchief, place his glasses over his hanky, and doze off. I never understood how he could sleep that way."

Abe Cruz recalls visits with Bibsy and Nonoy to Bambang's second-hand stores where they would buy clothes just for fun. "I remember Nonoy once bought a piece of cloth with zebra stripes. I thought he would use it to line his car. A few days later, he came to the office and there were the zebra stripes — on his pants." He was always wearing leather pants, says Anding Roces, "and they often ripped."

Such eccentricities are never put on — "There's nothing phony about him," says Roces. Abe Cruz describes him as a "liberated person." Cruz says that if Marcelo has changed at all, it is only in the sense that he has more money now. But Marcelo by his own admission has no respect for money; he doesn't even own a wallet. "Part *lang ng buhay pero hindi iyon ang* goal."

The goal for the present is still animation. If someone could give him a million pesos with which to produce a full-length animated film to celebrate the uniqueness of the Filipino, he would stay. In the meantime, he is busy enough with various activities — a column in *Expressweek* in which he gives full play to his brand of muddled, jumbled Taglish with the sort of irreverent humor his fans enjoy; a *Tisoy* movie being produced by Nora Aunor's film company and starring her husband, Christopher de Leon; plans for a geodesic dome to rise on a newly acquired piece of land at the foot of Mayon Volcano; a documentary on President Marcos for which Marcelo wrote the script; and, of course, *Aling* Otik the Metro Manila Aide. He is also painting and looks forward to aging, when he can sit outside his dome at the foot of Mayon and paint away.

The MG that he left behind when he took his longest coffee break is being refurbished according to his specifications. He feels lost in Manila without it and rarely ventures out alone. Sometimes, as he sits in his room, he wonders if people haven't been using him for their own ends. "Sucker *ako sa mga tao*," he says. His eyes burn momentarily at the thought that perhaps he has been used once too often. And then he remembers the friends he has, and he smiles.

Nonoy Marcelo has a built-in protection against bitterness or recrimination — he never regrets anything he has done, never has felt sorry, never apologizes. He admits to misdeeds, yes, and to close friends and those whose confidence he has gained he speaks candidly of loves and relationships he has won and lost. *"Sa bobits matagalan talaga, taunan."* With women he looks for meaningful relationships.

On this homecoming he has found that the people he has loved, the people of whose lives he was once a part, have gone their individual ways. There is a pattern in their lives now in which he has no place. He will leave well enough alone. He is not one to dwell on what could have been.

Goodman
February 1977

Nonoy Marcelo's hair has turned snow-white, but at age 56 he is raring to test new ground and fulfill old dreams. Recently, he did one of the latter, an animated film on the history of the Philippine flag for the Aguinaldo Shrine in Kawit, Cavite. The film stars Marcelo's popular cartoon character Ikabod the mouse, who also stars in the komiks *version of the making of the Malolos Constitution. Over the years, Marcelo has been art director and cartoonist of various newspapers and magazines* (Manila Chronicle, Manila Times, Evening Paper, Isyu, Hu!Ha!, Philippine Journalism Review, I magazine, Pinoy Times). *As a writer and cartoonist, he has produced Dagalandia Komiks, pocketbooks, a guide to elections, and an Ikabod long-play record and cassette tape. He has received three Catholic Mass Media Awards for best comic strip, a Manila Critics Circle book citation, a Great Son of Malabon award, a Golden Honor award, and two awards for most humorous cartoons from the Society of Philippine Illustrators and Cartoonists.*

Fernando Modesto's Erotica

Early this month, at the Cultural Center's museum hallway, Fernando Modesto is all set to exhibit framed paper bags on which he has painted stylized versions of the condom.

Modesto, you see, is hung up on the erotic.

In 1974, more out of playfulness than seriousness, one hopes, he put up a show at Shop 6 of Kamalig titled *"Ano ang* Feeling *ng Saging?"* The entire exhibition consisted of yellow bananas suspended from the ceiling, the artist's contribution to sculpture. Opening-night guests helped themselves to the fruits so that visitors on subsequent days had only banana peelings to ponder.

In 1975 Modesto made news with shows at the Rear Room Gallery and the Cultural Center of erotic and nonerotic drawings, the subjects of which were phalluses and tops, respectively. "Imagine an army of phalluses!" screamed one writer.

Modesto's voyage to erotica has taken him to Tokyo, where an exhibition of 150 of his drawings was organized in 1976 by two men who have become patrons of his works — a British banker named William Thurson and an Italian named Bruno Arkari. It was the second such private viewing of Modesto's erotic drawings set up by the pair, who until today, according to the artist, buy up whatever he produces.

WHO IS Fernando Modesto and why is he into phalluses and condoms?

Iskho Lopez once described him as the enfant terrible of local art circles who sports "long hair, a buck-toothed smile, a heart condition and ulcers to boot." That was almost four years ago, when the artist was 21. Modesto has since cut his hair short but the buck-toothed smile remains, as do the heart condition and the ulcers. He has also remained elfin-like at five feet.

Fernando Modesto

Modesto has a personal history as colorful as his condoms. He grew up in Caloocan with his maternal grandmother, a crippled old woman who in her prime had had six husbands, including, says Modesto, the mayor of a Luzon town. Modesto's mother was the last daughter from her last marriage. As a boy, he remembers being baptized in a river according to the rites of the Iglesia ni Cristo and rebaptized as a Catholic when he was adopted by an aunt at the age of 14.

Adolescence was to him a time for collecting, not girls, but urine — his — in bottles. And fingernails, also his. "I just wanted to see the color of the urine," he explains, as though it were as simple as that. His grandmother would be angry, of course, but she could not stop him. He eventually did "because the people around me couldn't take it." Today, if he had his wish, he would be collecting skulls.

Modesto is hard put trying to explain how and where he derived the eroticism in his art. "If my grandmother were alive today," he says sheepishly, "she would be shocked." His mother, whom he sees only twice or thrice a year, has no idea what her son is into, and he says that is for the better. Still, he offers no apologies for the kind of drawings that turn him on, delighting only in recalling that he once drew sperm graphs and someone bought the work without knowing what it was all about.

"Sex and freedom are universal themes," he maintains, and adds that they are what he wants to use as "guiding motives in my art." And, although the playfulness in his art somehow detracts from the seriousness with which he approaches it, he does hope that a decade from now he will be able to reach the stature of Chabet and Lee Aguinaldo, both of whom he admires for their energy.

If he did not have to work for a living, he says, he would be painting the whole day. Appropriately, after unhappy stints as poster artist for the Cultural Center and as textile designer for Evertex, he is now gainfully employed at the Population Center Foundation where his eroticism is not much in demand, but where people are at least not scandalized by his inordinate attachment to condoms.

Celebrity
March 15, 1979

Fernando Modesto moved with his family to Djakarta in 1986 and has since developed an international clientele for his art. He has mounted more than 60 one-man shows, not only in Manila but also in Madrid, Stockholm and Copenhagen. No longer into erotic art, he has become more introspective and spiritual of late, largely because of a recurring heart problem. He is married to advertising executive Eleanor San Jose and has two daughters.

Onib Olmedo
Sunshine Boy

Luis Olmedo, Jr. was his family's Bambino until he was three, when that pet name was shortened to Bino. Then, in the fashion of the day, his older brother took to spelling Bino backward. Onib it became and Onib it still is to this day, even on the artist's canvases.

Onib Olmedo grew up in a middle-class neighborhood in Manila's Sampaloc district, the fifth of 10 children of a Spanish *mestizo* couple. He remembers the Sampaloc of his childhood well: the children who lined the canals to catch *dapya,* the boys who set up basketball courts in the middle of the street, the floodwaters that rose almost as soon as the rains fell. It was a neighborhood where, occasional squabbles and verbal battles notwithstanding, people knew and liked one another.

Onib knew his neighbors well, not just the folks next door but even those several blocks away. Since 1971, when he first took up the brush, they have peopled his canvases: Gerry Kalawang the tough guy, Starlet O'Hara the woman who loved much and unwisely, Aw the feeble-minded ex-boxer, and many more. They appear in Onib's paintings as sometimes grotesque, oftentimes depressing, figures. Most people viewing Onib's works have cringed or turned away. Onib is familiar with such reactions; he is not a pretty-people, beautiful-landscape painter. He would like, he says, to be categorized as a humanist who confronts with his art, the way the early Bencab did, the way Danny Dalena, Pablo Baens Santos and Cesar Legaspi do now.

"All the reviews of my work emphasize the aspect of economic poverty," Onib says. "Actually, that forms a very small aspect of my paintings. I feel that spiritually the people in my paintings are on a higher level than most people I know. My people may look oppressed but they are not defeated — they have fortitude, are ready to fight back. What is depressing perhaps are the circumstances

ONIB OLMEDO

in which they live, but the persons themselves are able to endure or to rise above their situation."

Criticism of his work does not bother Onib much; neither, he says, does flattery. "If the person who criticized or praised my work turns out to be someone I respect, I would be affected by what he or she says. But if the praise comes from someone who has bad taste, *delikado pa.*"

He has learned his lesson well. Sometime ago he took one of his paintings to Taza de Oro, where the Saturday Group of artists, to which he belongs, used to meet. He was seeking criticism of his work from the painters who were gathered there. "No two comments," he recalls, "were alike. The best comment came from Malang who told me, *'Huwag mo silang intindihin. Kung susundin mo sila, magpipinta ka lang na kapareho nila.'"*

These days Onib is preparing for a one-man exhibition (scheduled to open on November 28), his fourth in seven years. Unlike other artists, he does not believe in exhibiting every year. "I planned to have a show last year but I felt the development was not definite enough. I don't put up a show for the sake of having one. An exhibition is supposed to show something new, and unless I have that I won't exhibit."

There *is* something new about Onib's forthcoming show. His subjects are still people — a *sakada,* a young prison inmate, a clairvoyant, a beer garden entertainer, a forgotten whore, among others — but "I am more concerned now with the mood of the painting." He describes some of his new works as surreal although he says the elements he puts together are not meant to be symbols. He explains:

"I used to have a particular situation, a particular person in mind. This time the person in the painting is not anybody in particular and I have no particular situation in mind. The person is not even an example of a type, only a medium to express a type.

"I put objects just to add to the mood. Several objects together create a certain feeling. The feelings in most of these new paintings are the same as those in my earlier works where I tried to convey the idea of poverty — economic and moral — and oppression and the harsh realities of life. My intention is to confront those realities so as to help people become more aware and less escapist."

Artists, Onib believes, have a responsibility to society, so that while he paints mainly to satisfy himself he also keeps in mind that his role as an artist in society is to be a catalyst, to make a social comment.

An architect by training (he placed among the top 10 in the government examinations for architects in the early Sixties), he practised his profession for 10 years until his partner left for the United States.

Finding himself frequently alone in the office, he turned to drawing. He had not drawn since his student days at Mapua, where he did cartoon strips for the school paper. This time an architect-friend who had just arrived from abroad saw Onib's drawings, was fascinated by them and insisted on taking them with him to the U.S. He shared his discovery with Onib's former partner who, equally fascinated, sent his old friend a set of oils.

That gift started Onib off on a new profession. He stopped seeking out or entertaining clients, and in 1973 gave up architecture altogether. His fantasies, however, remain architectural. Asked to describe his fantasy house, he says with a laugh, *"Ang dami na,* a different one each time. Sometimes my dream houses even contradict each other. *Minsan* towards nature — something organic that grew from nature. Sometimes totally man-made, sculptural, sleek."

"MY ART," Onib once confessed to a friend, "has enabled me to get rid of my complexes." He was a loner in his youth, a terribly shy boy who would go on Sunday excursions to the beach all by himself, reassured only by the presence in his pockets of a can of pork and beans and a can opener.

The shyness remains today, but only with strangers and casual acquaintances, with whom he seems to be uncomfortable and forever on his guard. With close friends, however, he is completely uninhibited. They speak of his generosity and warmth and honesty, but most of all, his sense of humor. Odette Alcantara, who runs Heritage Art Center in San Juan, is a self-confessed Onib fan. "He is my favorite kind of person, a terrific raconteur. Onib is not a first impressionist; he doesn't open up easily. He reveals himself to you little by little. But when you get to know him better, he is the exact opposite of your first impression of him."

Odette, who wears a specially printed Onib Fans Club T-shirt (as do the likes of Sylvana Diaz, Capt. Angel de Jesus and Lorna Montilla), looks forward to Onib's almost daily visits to Heritage, where he plays chess. *"Maski ano ang* mood *mo, pag dumating si* Onib, *he brings sunshine,"* she says.

Graphic designer Manny Arriola, a friend to Onib these past 16 years, concurs with Odette. "There is never a dull moment with Onib. It is hard to relate him to the kind of paintings he produces."

Onib says he inherited his funny bone from his parents. "Both of them had a sense of humor — my father's was wry, sophisticated, even sarcastic, quite British, while my mother's was simpler, more descriptive. It seems I got both brands."

The favorite target of Onib's own peculiar brand of humor is himself. He likes to recall the time two Spanish-looking ladies visited a Makati gallery and saw one of his paintings. Curious, he sidled up to them, only to be jolted by their horrified reaction to his work. One of the women exclaimed, "I wouldn't hang this goddamn thing in my toilet!" Forthwith, Onib took the painting home and hung it in his toilet, where it stayed for a while. It didn't look good there, he says, flashing his trademark grin.

Onib's two daughters, six-year-old Bambi and four-year-old Franjo, whom he puts to bed with a succession of nursery rhymes in Pilipino (which, says his wife Bettina, are either downright silly or slightly off-color) and fairy tales with the story lines all mixed up, have learned to turn the tables on their father. Once, while watching him at work, Bambi remarked, *"Ang galing mong gumawa ng pangit!"* Franjo, the more artistically inclined of the Olmedo offspring, chipped in her own comment, *"Baka mapanaginipan ko 'yan."* Very much her father's daughter, Franjo replies nonchalantly when he asks her to explain a painting or drawing of hers, *"Wala, basta maganda lang."*

The two girls enjoy watching their father paint and, says Onib, fight for possession of the finished work. This early, they are understandably partial to their father's paintings, despite their wisecracks about them. Onib himself admits his self-confidence has grown tremendously over the past few years. "I know more about art now. I used to get satisfied so easily. *Lahat ng makita ko dati* — my works as well as those of others — *nagagandahan ako. Lahat ng* exhibit *na puntahan ko, bilib na bilib ako. Ngayon, pakonti nang pakonti ang gusto ko.* But when I look at works now I can appreciate the intention behind them."

Still, his self-confidence fails him when he hears from gallery curators that his paintings are selling better now than before. "I don't know if that is because they really like me or they're just tired of the other artists," he quips. Odette Alcantara says most of Onib's works are bought by his fellow artists and foreigners more than by local patrons. She takes that as a good sign: "It shows his art is not localized."

"WHEN I PAINT," says Onib, "I don't have anything in mind. I try to keep my mind blank. That's why I am not successful every time. I actually finish only one out of every three paintings I start on."

"Onib works spontaneously," explains Manny Arriola. "That, I think, is the best way to put your whole being into whatever you are doing. Your work becomes more honest, more true to life."

"Art," says Onib, "should come out naturally. A lot of artists look for a style first and try to express themselves through that style instead of trying to express what they like."

"Onib," says his friend Manny, "is concerned with content where other artists are more preoccupied with form, color and shape."

Arriola singles out Onib's compassionate eye as an artist. Only someone who observes and studies human nature closely, Manny believes, can paint with the understanding and compassion with which Onib depicts his character. Onib does his people-watching in some of Metro Manila's busiest districts: Sampaloc, Quiapo, Ermita and the San Lazaro Hippodrome, where he is a judge and steward (as his grandfather and his father had been). He says, "I used to observe the lonely people in Quiapo's restaurants. They would sit hunched over a table full of empty beer bottles, just waiting for someone to smile and show some interest in them. Those people would grab at a chance to talk with anybody."

Just outside Quiapo Church, Onib would stop to listen to informal debates between characters he came to know as Fundamental (so-called because he was always using that word), Paos, Fidel Castro (a beggar who wore an army uniform) and Kapatid.

Today, however, Onib prefers to take his long walks in Ermita. It is to Mabini he hies off after an early morning round of tennis in a La Loma court. Plaza Ferguson along Roxas Boulevard is a favorite hangout, for there he meets chess nuts like himself, an odd assortment of characters who include newsmen, retired policemen, drivers, musicians and barbers. They offer him not only chess but also a wealth of experiences told as anecdotes, Onib's kind of conversation. "I enjoy their company," he says. "They are so down-to-earth, have no pretensions whatsoever."

When lunchtime catches him in Ermita he goes to a small eatery that, he says, is patronized by broke Mabini artists. The place is small and cramped, *"pero may* jukebox." And the cook has pretensions to being himself an artist. Going about shirtless but always with a beret perched on his head, the man serves his customers, says Onib, all the while doing a mean Travolta.

"Iba-iba ang tao, mas masarap kausap," he explains his preference for Ermita. In contrast, he says, Makati might be great for girl-watching after lunch "but the people are either not interesting *o hindi* interested *sa akin."* When he has seen all the current exhibitions in Makati's many galleries, he seeks refuge at the Front Room, actor Nestor de Villa's cozy restaurant at the Makati Commercial Center. Onib takes a table by the window — the better, he jokes, to see the girls passing by. He has learned to play backgammon at the Front Room, and to one's question-cum-comment (Why backgammon? Isn't that a *burgis* pastime?) he protests that no one there plays chess.

Now it's his turn to shoot a question-cum-comment. *"Celebrity?* I hope your magazine doesn't make me a celebrity. I don't quite like the connotation of that word."

"*Burgis,*" he echoes fellow artist Tiny Nuyda, who has joined him at the table. And Onib closes the backgammon set.

"Nothing," declares his friend Manny later, "can make Onib Olmedo *burgis.*"

Celebrity
September 15, 1981

Onib Olmedo won two gold medals as a figurative expressionist in the Art Association of the Philippines' annual competitions (1978 and 1981), a gold in the Mobil Art Awards contest (1980), an Araw ng Maynila award (1991), a CCP Thirteen Artists award (1992) and honorable mention in the Internationale Exposition des Peintures in France (1992). His works were exhibited not only in the Philippines but also in France, Holland, Germany, the U.S., Iraq, Guam and Austria. In 1994 he was elected as the first chair of the Saturday Group of artists executive committee. On September 8, 1996 art circles were stunned to learn that he had suffered a stroke and died. He was 59 years old.

Boots Anson-Roa
Somebody Human

It must be tough being Boots Anson-Roa.

It must be tough having to prove, in these days when public relations can do wonders for just about anybody who can afford it, that the smile is genuine, the intelligence profound, the compassion sincere. And to prove that yes, it is possible, in these troubled and troublesome times, to adhere to one's childhood values and not be dismissed as an anachronism.

And yet Boots Anson-Roa, while admitting to feeling flattered by her public image of "perfect wife and mother, good girl, living angel," prefers to be described as "somebody human," as having, like everyone else, a vulnerable side.

Her father, the former Sampaguita movie actor Oscar Moreno. says of his firstborn: "She's one in a billion."

There must surely be an element of subjectivity in that fatherly statement, so perhaps we could settle for "one in a million"?

MA. ELISA ANSON was, her father recalls, a "very serious child who was quite mature for her age." The eldest of four children, she was named after her paternal grandmother, who was three-fourths Spanish, and nicknamed Boots after a comic strip character in the Forties.

"There are children you have to nag every day," says Moreno, "but not Boots. She was such a good girl. She knew right from wrong at a very early age. And she was always interested in people. When my friends came to see me at home, she would entertain them while I got dressed. She was never shy, never awkward."

School was St. Paul College at first, and then Assumption Convent, which was much closer to the Anson home on Dakota Street in Malate. She was to stay there until her graduation from

BOOTS ANSON-ROA

high school. Lila Quirino, who was Boots's gangmate in high school, remembers her friend as *"mabait na magulo,* very active in social work, always *makuwento,* a very good daughter. She never forgot anyone she met, not even our maids." At Assumption Boots excelled not only in class but also in co-curricular activities. She was an honor student, an excellent warball player, an officer of the class and of the school chapter of Student Catholic Action, and an active member of the drama club.

Oscar Moreno remembers his daughter's high school graduation ceremony well. "She was the youngest in the graduating class — 14 going on 15. She got so many medals that another father behind me commented, 'What is this, a monopoly of your daughter?'" Moreno chuckles at the memory.

He did not want his daughter in the movies, not yet anyway. The Vera-Perezes of Sampaguita had been eyeing her for years but her father demanded that she get an education first. He did not, he told her, want history to repeat itself. He himself had only three semesters to go of the foreign service course at the University of the Philippines when the opportunity to become a movie star came his way, and he could not reject it. He did not want his daughter to have any regrets.

She did not let him down.

From Assumption she went to U.P. for speech and drama, carrying on, in all the four years she was at the state university, the standards of excellence she had already set for herself. One leafs through her albums today and sees photographs of her receiving a scholarship citation from U.P. president Carlos P. Romulo, taking her oath as president of the Women's Club, leading other coeds in a walkathon she initiated, posing with other stalwarts of the U.P. theater group, smiling during the traditional Cadena de Amor festival, standing at attention as a corps sponsor, and so on and so forth. There was never time put to waste or even time to be silly.

"PAG SERIOUS pala masyado ang isang tao, pag pumasok ang kalokohan sa ulo, tuluy-tuloy. Nagulat ako sa sarili ko."

Boots Anson-Roa is talking of the circumstances that led to her marriage 15 years ago. The marriage was precipitated by a dare. The young man was Pete Roa, who was hosting, together with Baby O'Brien, a television program called *Dance-O-Rama*. Baby eventually left the show to get married and Channel 5 went around the school campuses in search of a replacement for her. The U.P. administration suggested Boots Anson, who said no the first time the idea was broached to her. But the Channel 5 representatives were persistent, and faced with the prospect of on-the-job training plus an attractive salary, she changed her mind.

Roa courted his new co-emcee, to the delight of *Dance-O-Rama* viewers who sighed each time he opened the show with a rose for her, plucked, she says with a laugh today, from the bouquet meant for that day's queen. The courtship lasted all of six months, after which they sought permission to marry. Belen Cristobal-Anson, who was by this time separated from her actor-husband, refused to give them her blessings. Like other parents of talented offspring, she had her own dreams for Boots: a trip abroad, a master's degree perhaps. Oscar Moreno had his own objection to the young man his daughter fancied: Pete was, he thought, too much of a man of the world for his daughter.

The columnist Jose L. Guevara takes credit for the couple's elopement. He had seen them at a Caltex party on June 3 and, knowing the real score between them, had teased, *"Magtanan na kayo."* They took it in good humor that night, but the following morning, over the phone, they found themselves daring each other to carry out Guevara's challenge.

"I did not feel a tinge of fear," says Boots. Instead of going to Baguio, which was the favorite hideout of eloping couples, they hied off to Ma Mon Luk for some *siopao* and then to Little Quiapo for *halo-halo*. They had hoped to get a marriage license from Quezon City Mayor Norberto Amoranto, but His Honor was celebrating a birthday and they were told to return the next day. They passed the night at the home of Pete's sister-in-law—one unmarried night, says Boots, which necessitated a premarital confession to a priest. But first to Mayor Amoranto again, whom they joined for breakfast the next morning and who joined them together as man and wife in the presence of late-coming well-wishers. In the afternoon they went to see the late Father

Veneracion, rowdy Leveriza's "hoodlum" priest, who heard their confessions and then breezed through the marriage ceremony.

The Roas have no photographs of their wedding day; the neighborhood photographer summoned by Father Veneracion had forgotten to load his camera. That was not the only humorous sidelight to their quickie of a wedding: the mattress Pete's mother salvaged from the *bodega* for the newlyweds to use that evening was, says Boots, so infested with bedbugs they spent their wedding night getting rid of the bloodsuckers.

The couple stayed with the elder Roas for a year before going off on their own.

"ONE OF THE THINGS I emphasize when I am asked to speak on love and marriage is for people not to think that Pete and I are a perfect couple. There is no such thing."

Boots says, however, that she did resolve to make her marriage work as her parents' own did not. "I told myself whatever mistakes I had seen in my folks' marriage I'd try to avoid. Whatever void they had in their marriage I'd try to fill in my own. When a marriage breaks up, both parties are to blame."

For a time she was simply wife to Pete and mother to Leah and Joey, who were born a year apart. Until Virgo producer Liza Moreno called, offering her a role opposite Eddie Rodriguez in *El Perro Gacho,* an action drama. Boots turned down the offer. A determined Liza called again and again, each time making her offer more attractive.

"*Sige,* I said, one-shot deal. Pete and I talked about it. He said he foresaw what would happen. Acting was, after all, in my blood, so I just had to be prepared for what was in the offing. What mattered most to me was whether or not Pete approved. But then, as now, Pete has never said no to anything I ask his advice about. He never categorically says no. He never imposes."

Her husband had read the signs correctly. That one-shot deal in 1968 led to another and another, until acting became her profession. In the early days, Boots recalls, a number of producers suggested she drop the Roa from her screen name. She refused, explaining she wanted to give her husband the importance he deserved. Boots Anson-Roa is too long a name, people told her. The producers also suggested she play down in her press interviews the fact that she was a married woman. In the past no woman who entered the movies already married had made it. She was told she was courting disaster if she insisted on her way.

"I said let the fans take me for what I am. It will be just too bad for me if they don't like married women in showbiz. I told the producers okay *lang,* I'll be in the business for only a few years, but my family is for a lifetime."

To the producers' surprise, and Boots's too, the public welcomed her with open arms. She explains their response very simply: "The family was the angle that set me apart from the rest." The fact that she had a husband and children served another useful purpose: it became what Boots calls "an invisible protective membrane" that kept in their place male predators who had less than honorable designs. She talks of one leading man who showed her special attention, actually articulating his feelings. The Roas, who both believe that the "best weapon against bad intentions is to show the person you trust him," made the man their *kumpadre.*

Most of her male co-stars, however, treat Boots like a sister, solicitously looking after her needs when they are shooting, being, in general, very attentive and affectionate. In particular she cites Joseph Estrada, who is also a *kumpadre* but not for the same reason as the actor mentioned earlier. Estrada has gone on record as saying Boots is his lucky charm. Twice during the last eight years, his production outfit suffered reversals and it took a picture starring himself and Boots to take the company out of the red. In 1971 Boots made four consecutive Erap comedies with Estrada, all of them box-office hits. This year, after three dismal flops, Estrada asked Boots to do *Warrant of Arrest* with him. The formula worked again. An elated Estrada sent to the Roa house one Sunday morning, a few days after *Warrant* opened in the theaters, four huge cakes and a bottle of Chivas Regal Royal Salute. The note that accompanied the presents went, "Lifesavers are not only candy flavors, they're also people like you."

The Roas' friendship with Estrada is one of the few social links they maintain in the movie industry. It is not only because they have not much time for socializing, says Boots, but because she has always believed in a sense of detachment. "You have to be," she explains, "a superwoman to be very attached to the industry in a totality and detach yourself from its surplus demands. That is why the really big successes — if by success you mean reaching the zenith of popularity and earning the maximum — are the ones who have been swallowed by it, who really have succumbed to its demands at the expense of their personal values, their time, their privacy, their principles."

After 11 years and 70 movies, Boots is still not the superstar that Nora and Vilma are. Not that she has ambitions of becoming one. Contrary to what people think, she is not in the P100,000 bracket — yet. *"Ang katwiran ko, pwede nga akong humingi noon, matagal na dapat, pero may* demands *iyan. Pag humingi ka ng* P100,000, you have to give P100,000 worth of your time and attention beyond what is professionally called for. And I'm not willing to do that. I am willing to give only the professional in me — so I emcee for free, join fund-raising campaigns for the movies, etc. But the other demands, those that approach exploitation, I don't care for."

The nonfinancial rewards from the industry have come without her having to try too hard. In 1974, the year she considers her peak (before the bold trend eased virginal actresses like her out of the screen), she was named "Queen of Philippine Movies" by a board of judges. And there was the FAMAS award for best actress that she shared with Vilma Santos. This year, to Boots's astonishment, she was named by the movie press one of their "10 darlings." "I can look anybody straight in the eye," she says, "because I have never lobbied for any award, or sweet-talked anybody, or made any under-the-table deals."

At 34, Boots feels she has reaped too many laurels too early, not the least of which is inclusion among the Ten Outstanding Women of the Philippines when she was 29. It was the first time a national award was given to a movie actress. She is grateful for such recognition but even more appreciative of the support she receives from her husband.

"Pete is a very rare kind of person. It is hard to see his goodness if you don't know him well enough. He is very unselfish, at least

I think it is unselfishness to let your wife go this far and attain all this. He has never stood in my way or even minded staying behind. I think if I had been married to someone else, someone who would not give me as much leeway as Pete has, I would not be where I am now. It takes a very confident person to do that."

Pete Roa has been addressed, whether innocently or maliciously, as Mr. Anson or Mr. Anson-Roa. His wife concedes that such incidents could prick the male ego but do not ruffle her husband. What they succeed in doing is to make her more conscientious about her role as a wife, so that even today she bothers to prepare coffee for Pete even when she is in a rush to go somewhere, looks into his closets for clothes that need darning, and hands him his slippers at night.

"I cannot afford to be spoiled," she says. *"Hindi ba,* the Pope kisses the ground. Maybe if I were an ordinary wife, I would be spoiled." On the other hand, she is also aware of the pitfalls of being too efficient, of being, like a true Aquarian, too independent. "People like to feel needed. When I ask Pete to do little things for me, they are purposely done. We like the feeling of having done something for somebody. Otherwise, I am very independent.

"Wala kaming bickering, *talagang wala. Tampo, siyempre. Sama ng loob, siyempre meron.* But there is never any head-on collision. When Pete sees that I'm about to burst, he will tell me to go to the children's room or we'll talk about it later. We talk about our problem the day after, or we go out on a date — to dinner and a movie. *Nagkukwentuhan kami ng sama ng loob, pero naka-*candlelight *naman."*

"WHEN I LISTEN to some mothers complain about their children, I realize how lucky I am."

The four Roa children — 14-year-old Leah, 13-year-old Joey, 9-year-old Chiqui and 6-year-old Benjo — learned early enough that their mother must be shared with other people. Share, says Boots, is a key word in her family. "They seem to have assimilated that idea very well and so far there have been no complaints." One day recently, the children were asked by their parents to write down what they liked most about their mother and their father and what they liked least. Boots says she and Pete were prepared for the worst, such as expressions of deep-seated resentments. Their fears proved groundless, however, for the children, Boots says amusedly, wrote the silliest things, like "Mommy has *patay na buhok*" and *"mahirap magpaalam kay* Mommy" and "Daddy is easier to ask for beyond-the-budget groceries."

"I exert extra effort," says Boots of her parenting style. "The children can see that I try to make it up to them." Before she started her new early-morning show on television, *Kung Kami Ang Tatanungin,* she would get up at six in the morning, even when she had been shooting overnight or taping till four a.m., to have breakfast with the children before they rushed off to school. These days, she wakes up at five, but there is time only to check whether the children have their lunch boxes and allowances, and then she is off to the studio. She still makes it a point, though, to attend the children's school functions, no matter how trivial, and to cheer them on in their studies. (Both girls are in the honor roll at Maryknoll; at the Ateneo, Benjo is a top student and Joey a promising artist.)

Although obviously privileged, the children get their fair share of discipline. "There are times," says their mother, "when they ask for something we can afford but I say not now. It is good for them to be frustrated once in a while, to know how it is to be deprived, to hunger for something. We hardly spank them. We believe in the soft, firm word but we do believe in punishment, which takes the form of either kneeling in front of the statue of Sto. Niño and praying, or ostracizing them, making them feel how it is to be alone and to have no friends. Policing oneself is another keyword with the children. We want them to keep from doing things not out of fear, but because they don't want to offend. On holidays they're supposed to wash their own dishes, but sometimes they forget. I learned early, from my parents and the nuns, that whatever I can do by myself, *huwag nang iutos sa iba."*

"I ALWAYS TELL Pete, I'd rather wear out than rust out."

A self-confessed workaholic, Boots laughingly recalls that she actually woke up one morning and, as is her habit, started to say her morning prayer. What she said, however, was, "Good morning, Jesus, and welcome to the show." When absentmindedness does not get the better of her, though, her morning prayer consists of gratitude for the previous night and meditation on what she is supposed to do on this new day.

"My greatest accomplishment and sense of achievement," she says, "is derived from work. Someone told me once that I live to work, not the other way around. But the fact is, I feel sick when I'm not doing anything. I'm very work-oriented. In school we were told not to waste time. *Baka nagkamali ako ng* interpretation, *na* if you're not moving, you're idle. I guess I went to the other extreme."

That "other extreme" involves films (she is back in circulation after lying low for a year), television *(Kapwa Ko, Mahal Ko,* where she is on twice a week, and *Kung Kami Ang Tatanungin,* which is aired five times a week), radio (a daily talk show on Radio Veritas), a garments factory, a restaurant (which her father and her uncle manage) and lecture engagements (she receives an average of six invitations a week from students, clubs, civic organizations). This year she went on leave from the Zonta Club, an all-female group in which membership is strictly by invitation. She still makes herself available, however, for fund-raising projects which need her name and influence.

Her Radio Veritas show and *Kapwa Ko, Mahal Ko* she considers part of her apostolate, the remunerations from them being more of honoraria. "You cannot," she says, "equate everything with money. I meet a lot of people on those shows who say they pray for me and my family."

Orly Mercado of *Kapwa Ko, Mahal Ko* speaks of Boots's "very pronounced common touch, her sensitivity to the needs and feelings of other people." Indeed, the two-year-old brick-walled Roa home in Loyola Heights is, according to the man of the house, a branch of the Department of Social Welfare. "I'm very gullible," says Boots. "People come to the house asking for help and I can't turn them away. I used to find it so difficult to say no. *Pag humindi ako,* I felt I was being very selfish. But a priest told me I have to develop my perspectives, I'm not Wonder Woman."

WHEN BOOTS speaks of herself today, it is in terms of before and after Russia. Early this year she visited the Soviet Union on a cultural mission with Nestor Torre, Jr. and Tommy Abuel. The trip gave her a chance to introspect, to develop her perspectives, as her priest-friend had counseled her.

"When I was in Russia I told Nestor, 'Come to think of it. I've always had a live-and-let-live attitude.' And then I realized my attitude was let-live *lang,* walang live. I'm very strict with myself but very lenient and liberal with other people, including Pete. But with myself I have too many self-imposed restrictions. Some people say they have to learn to say no to themselves. *Ako naman, baliktad.* So, after Russia, I said, I will live!"

Her first step in that direction was to learn to smoke. "I said, I'm growing old, I should have at least one vice. Pete says *pakitang tao lamang ito.* Maybe it's a rebellion against my self-imposed restrictions, but the important thing is I'm enjoying it." Even then she limits herself to four or five sticks a day; some days she does not smoke at all.

In Russia, too, she learned to drink. She had never liked the taste of wine before. Pete would treat her to a fancy dinner and to his chagrin she would ask for a soft drink to go with fried chicken or spaghetti. Today, thanks to numerous vodka toasts in Russia, she says she is starting to like red wine, and at the Barnyard, the family-owned restaurant off Makati Avenue, she has learned to take one or even two Margaritas.

At the professional level, the Russian experience helped Boots develop more mature attitudes towards portrayals. She had been, she realized, too image-conscious in choosing her roles. Even before Russia, though, she had made a start towards loosening up with her off-beat role in the play *The Owl and the Pussycat,* but then having Pete for her leading man made the transition easier. Post-Russia, she accepted the role of the free spirit in Lino Brocka's restaging of Nick Joaquin's *Mga Ama, Mga Anak.* The play was a turning point for Boots. "One line struck me most in the play." she says. "I had this line that went *'Hindi tayo dapat mas mahigpit sa ating sarili kaysa sa Diyos.' Sabi ko, tamang-tama sa akin."*

She considers herself fortunate to be aware of her imperfections. "After awareness," she tells herself, "comes the effort to correct myself." Now she would like to work towards "relaxing more and not feeling guilty about it." That should not be too difficult to do for someone who has always tried to overcome negative feelings — shame, fear, anger — and for someone who has often tried, successfully, to outdo herself.

In the final analysis, however, it is faith that sustains Boots Anson-Roa. "I don't know what you could call it," she says, reacting to one's suggestion of a hotline up there. "I have everything that matters, the essentials in life, and even some of the nonessentials. I just pray for two things: that I know what He wants me to do and that I'm equipped with whatever I need to do it."

Surely, she gets all she needs, and more.

Celebrity
November 30, 1979

Boots Anson-Roa was appointed chair, president and general manager of Intercontinental Broadcasting Corporation (IBC-13) in July 1998 by newly elected President Joseph Estrada, her former leading man. Before that appointment, she was vice president for the television division of Premiere Entertainment Productions, Inc. Boots was away for 11 years starting in 1981, when she accepted a job at the Philippine Embassy in Washington, D.C., as press attache, cultural officer and special assistant to the ambassador. From 1986 until she and Pete returned to Manila in 1993, she worked in various companies and took several certificate courses. Upon her return, she resumed her acting career and hosted a number of TV shows. She and Pete now have six grandchildren.

Alfredo Roces
The Artist as Person

The house in Pasay, on a street that was quiet and modestly genteel until it was invaded by Chinese millionaires and Manila-bound jeepneys, looks old and unpretentious. It is an old house, acquired by its owner even before his marriage in the mid-Fifties from an American expatriate who was being recalled home. And it is unpretentious, except for the presence of a dour-faced, blue-uniformed guard who screens all visitors at the gate. The security man is somehow out of character with this house, whose owner has never concealed his disdain for all forms of elitism.

But Alfredo R. Roces, whose house it is, settles one's momentary confusion about what seems to be a discrepancy between his lifestyle and his personal conviction. The guard, he explains, is a recent acquisition, made necessary by two unrelated incidents of trespassing on the Roces property, the second rendered hilarious by the fact that the only weapon he could find in his houseful of antiques was a spear to fight off the gun-wielding intruders. The thieves ran away empty-handed, scared off not by the spear but by the unexpected sight of the master of the house himself. And Roces, properly warned, did what any peace-loving family man who can afford to buy security would do. He hired a guard, the reality of whose presence he must still learn to live with.

Roces, one finds, is a very open person. The clear brown eyes have an earnest look about them, and even the beard which he has had on and off (mostly on) since his college days is not the kind that intimidates, but rather looks as though it were born with him. The cheeks that used to be full, chubby almost, have stretched out, and with his thinner face he is starting to look, at 44, like his elder brother Alejandro. The voice gives him away: it is

ALFREDO R. ROCES

high-pitched, unmistakably Roces, though less pronouncedly so. What does not give him away so easily is his slight build, coupled with a somewhat stooped frame, which quite effectively hides the fact that Alfredo Roces — artist, writer, editor, art critic — is also quite a sportsman.

The inner toughness underneath the frail physique was acquired in childhood, for Roces is the youngest of nine children, all of them male. Very early in life he developed a facility for asking questions, not only out of curiosity but out of a sense of self-preservation. His natural curiosity and keenly developed critical faculty served him well during his 10 years as *Manila Times* daily columnist, but in his younger days those were traits not exactly appreciated within the family circle. "Being No. 9 raised my critical faculty up by nine points. The elder citizen had certain seniority privileges over the truth. That made me a little more inclined to question and to reject things." He was, even then, the unconventional sort.

SOMEONE like him would hardly have been tolerated for very long in an atmosphere of rigid conformity. When he reached second year at the Ateneo High School, he failed English composition. There was nothing wrong with his English but, he says as he laughs about the incident now, "I don't think the priests liked me." His teachers were young Jesuit scholastics who didn't inspire too much confidence in their competence.

Roces's natural curiosity and habitually questioning mind may have been taken for cockiness and youthful insolence. For one thing, he couldn't play along with the "silly things" he and his classmates were constantly being made to do, such as when they were told to write a short story: "This was 1946, 1947, just after the war, and nobody in our house owned a typewriter and I had to go ask my cousin in Oroquieta to type the story. We lived in Pasay then. My story came up to two pages, typed single space. The priest said it had to be five pages. I said I couldn't add any more. He insisted I had to add 200 words on the spot. I refused."

He also refused to go back to Ateneo and its "confining type of education." Instead he finished high school at Far Eastern

University, which was founded by his mother's brother. He found FEU "a different experience — you could do what you liked there and I found that more to my liking." The years spent at a nonsectarian school taught him a basic axiom he still holds dear today: "You do what you have to do. Nobody's going to tell you to do it. Everything I've done I've done because I liked to do it. I've never done something because somebody pressured me into doing it."

Even his inclination towards the arts came naturally, though with tremendous assistance from his father. Rafael F. Roces was not only a general businessman — he brought back from the United States the first jalousie windows after the war, built the Ideal Theater, set up the first gasoline station in Manila and the first sporting goods store, owned a ranch in Mindanao, mines in Palawan and interests in Santa Clara Lumber — but also an art patron. His youngest son's earliest recollections of works of art are of those in his parents' home, among them Felix Resurreccion Hidalgo's *Artista y Modelo*, a huge painting that is considered one of the artist's best; a portrait of a Roces ancestor by Lorenzo Guerrero; and watercolors by Fernando Amorsolo.

But these were not the only form of artistic exposure the older Roces gave his son. At 14, Alfredo started to take art lessons from Dominador Castañeda and, when he was much older, was introduced by his father to the master himself, Amorsolo, about whom Alfredo Roces would later write a book. Through his father, too, he met Don Alfonso Ongpin who at one time, Roces recalls, "held the culture of the Philippines in his hands." Ongpin was the best and biggest collector of all art in the country, a very generous man, Roces says, who would thrust into his reluctant hands a Luna or an Hidalgo each time he came for a visit. To Roces's regret today, he never accepted the proffered gifts.

At his father's urging, Roces went to the U.S. for college studies, starting out in Liberal Arts at the University of Notre Dame. Ironically, Rafael Roces was not too keen about having an artist for a son. But in Alfredo's first year at Notre Dame he joined a campus competition for watercolor paintings and his entry won a silver star. Encouraged, he decided to major in fine arts and minor in philosophy and for five years worked so seriously at honing his art that he didn't even think of coming home during the summer. The fine arts degree wasn't enough; he went on to New York for another year of training.

But whatever high expectations he had for a career in art were dashed when he came home in the mid-Fifties. "I realized how little people knew about art. I read some of the reviews being written and said, 'My God!' It wasn't just the avant garde thing that they weren't being advanced enough in; they weren't even giving a proper perspective on the past." Someone, he felt, had "to say something sane," and that was how he got drafted into the unlikely career of teaching and, eventually, writing.

Setting aside his brush while he concentrated on what he considered more urgent business, he accepted an invitation to teach the humanities and art appreciation at FEU, where his brother Alejandro was dean of the College of Liberal Arts and also headed a research team that was to develop the *sarimanok* and arouse public interest in the then unknown Moriones and Ati-atihan festivals. At FEU, the young professor set up a humanities club and for a time was in charge of the university paper, *The Advocate,* until a conflict with the administration on the issue of campus press freedom put an end to both his moderating and his teaching. Of those idealistic years, he says, "It was a fine experience, but it took a lot out of me."

BY THIS TIME, he had found another outlet for his frustration — the dismal state of art criticism in his country. Alejandro Roces had become secretary of education in the Macapagal administration and had ceased to write his daily column, "Roces and Thorns," in the *Manila Times*. His youngest brother welcomed the chance to write: "I got into writing and teaching for the same thing — something had to be done." At first he was "more concerned about art but that was not possible in a paper with as wide a circulation as the *Times.*" Neither did the paper take kindly to his request for a box where he could alternate a column with a caricature, a drawing or a cartoon. And so he began to appear as a daily columnist commenting primarily on art and culture at the start but gradually including politics, too.

As a columnist, Roces made no attempt at being highbrow ("I'm not very cerebral. I tend to incline towards intuition as a very basic motivation") but he always backed up his contentions with solid facts and a background in Philippine sociology. Between the light banter and "corn" dished out by Jose L. Guevara, the hysterical pronouncements of Teodoro F. Valencia and the political gossip of Maximo Soliven, more discriminating readers tended to prefer Roces's sober, intelligent commentary. This preference was borne out by the Citizens Council for Mass Media and the local government of Pasay, both of which honored Roces with awards for his brand of journalism.

Keeping up a daily column for 10 years was hectic and the reward was hardly monetary ("There was no money in it; I was getting P20 a day at the *Times*"), but it was "a chance to grow, like teaching." Now that he had his column, even his paintings, which had become gloomy and ponderous, developed "a more playful mood."

But he also made enemies as an art critic — the Art Association of the Philippines, Purita Kalaw Ledesma, Pura Santillan Castrence, the sculptor Napoleon Abueva, among others. "It's very difficult to be an artist and an art critic at the same time. You knock a few judges, a few friends, and they knock you back and it hurts." But he has also helped advance the career of many a young artist. "You keep pushing people and finally you realize you're the last in the line," he says, chuckling.

Ding Roces is far from being last in the line of contemporary Filipino artists, but as he himself points out without rancor, "A lot of people have made it overnight. I've never been an overnight wonder." True, there have been major awards from the AAP, the latest an Artist of the Year citation announced in December 1975, the reason for which he still has to discover. But then he has also been screened out of competition, the last time two years ago. Yet, "I am a very competitive person. I don't mind losing. Some artists become smug once they reach a certain stage in their career and don't dare compete for fear of losing. I'm not like that."

He adds: "Competitions are flukes, that's what many people don't realize. I've had so much experience at judging art contests, I can tell you the results are purely whimsy. They're a very human activity, after all, as our young painters should realize. Of course, contests are good because they develop competition, but one shouldn't take them too seriously." He recalls one particular contest in which he was a judge. "I didn't make it to the place of competition on time and when I got there, the rest of the judges had already screened the entries. Just so it wouldn't be said that I hadn't done anything, I looked around and saw this entry in a corner and put it in with the other judges' choices. It won second or third prize, I don't remember."

What perhaps spells the difference between Alfredo Roces and most other artists today is that while the latter are driven by a passion to achieve greatness, Ding Roces wants to be, not great or famous, but authentic. "I do not have this urgency to have a great name. Mine is a personal expression, a personal journey. I want to be real, to be me." Painting alone does not give him complete satisfaction, thus "I don't feel a strong motivation to really do many paintings."

Roces's unorthodox views on art undoubtedly alienate those who have more conventional thoughts on the subject. "Art is overblown nowadays. Today, the artist plays a priestly role. One's name is not important, was not for centuries until the Renaissance came along. Most of art was anonymous. The idea of appending too much egoism to the arts is something I renounce. The 'I' in art has gotten to such a point that the artist makes a big thing about 'my style, my expression.' Nanding Ocampo (artist Hernando R. Ocampo) and I have had discussions on this and we agree on one point: art is not quite so important as man. You cannot be a good artist unless you're a good man."

One of the Philippines' more articulate artists, Roces thrives on discussion and says of his colleagues who believe that their works should speak for themselves, "They are just hiding a sensitive skin. They don't want to be open to attack."

HIS OWN ART has undergone significant changes through the years. As a young man, he was partial to pastel and watercolor, then became fascinated by oils done with a palette knife. Towards the close of the Fifties, he began to see the "great potential of eclectic means in art." That was when objects, or pieces of junk, as some people would prefer to call them, came into a Roces picture. "Any material is art and any object is beautiful, depending on how one adapts one's framework or viewpoint." And so one finds on a Roces canvas a piece of driftwood, shells, porcelain, a sardine can, campaign buttons from the premartial law era. "Objects evoke experience in a person. I try to transform an object so that it acquires new organization and meaning." At the same time, he says he deliberately puts incongruous things together in a painting.

His is not a contrived playfulness but rather a childlikeness that delights in perceiving new designs and discovering endless possibilities for all kinds of material. His studio at home is cluttered with "junk" he has accumulated through the years: shells and fossils picked up on regular trips to Matabungkay beach in Batangas, *anting-anting,* a purple apple crate whose design particularly fascinates him, even a bottleful of wood shavings believed to relieve women of their menstrual pains, which caught his eye because of the way the shavings fell into place.

The picture window along the stairway of his home is lined with bottles of all shapes and sizes, for which he hopes someday to find the right glue to make a totem sculpture. The indoor pond boasts a collection of rocks hauled in from Montalban and Matabungkay. And in his office in Malate is an Ifugao bird cage from which, to one's wonderment, he pulls out and unfolds a large crumpled piece of paper filled with a drawing of birds in flight. The paper is lovingly folded again and just as lovingly returned to its cage.

"I don't know why I do things like this," the artist says. "It's just how I feel about certain things. Some friends give me all kinds of junk; they think of me when they find something. I have candy boxes filled with little objects, books that are not books but drawings and paintings. I collect many things: *anting-anting,* pre-historic pottery, baskets, *santos,* drawings (the hobby dates back to his boyhood and his collection is now tucked away in a portfolio: 'I look them over at night and I'm happy'). I doodle on certain materials; it's a compulsion."

TO SOMEONE with Roces's insatiable curiosity and sense of wonder, life cannot but be exciting. And it is, "especially at this stage when things are going on in Philippine art." Life was not always so exciting, however, for once upon a very long time ago, Roces was cynical (an aftermath of the war, he says) and quarrelsome. But the cynicism was short-lived and the violent fistfights that were a great part of his college years have become things of the past.

His mind today is forever preoccupied with one project or another — a brochure on Hernando Ocampo which he would like to expand into a book as a companion piece to his Amorsolo bestseller; a manuscript recently completed, dealing with a study of the human figure in Philippine art; a biographical novelette on Jose Rizal's four-year stay in Dapitan; a book on Filipino ethnic art; a culture desk to be introduced by a regional news agency.

There is a tempting offer to go to Australia and produce an encyclopedia of the world that will be heavy on Southeast Asian material. The offer comes on the heels of *Filipino Heritage,* the 10-volume, three-year encyclopedic project of which he was editor in chief. His work as *Heritage* editor called for intensive and extensive research on the Philippines from prehistoric times to 1946; it was a complete course in itself, a job after Roces's own heart, as is the new offer from Paul Hamlyn Pty. Ltd., also the publisher of *Heritage.* "It will be a chance to grow, not only for myself but for my family as well," he muses.

Personal and professional growth Roces has always attained in a state of economic independence. "I have tried to be economically free by taking all kinds of odd jobs (which have included a brief, unhappy experience in advertising). A lot of people follow the bohemian idea that if one wants to be a painter, one should not live off society, one should just starve in the gutter. I don't believe in that. If you want to be free to paint, you must be as economically free as possible. It is not possible to opt for starvation when you have a family to think about. I want to feel I've fed my family."

His family includes his wife Irene (nee Pineda) and three daughters — Mina, 16; Grace Maria, 15; and Maria Irene or Mia,

12. Mrs. Roces, who was working for a master's degree in business at Columbia University in New York when she met her future husband, is "a stabilizing force." While Roces has "always just done what I've felt like doing and followed my intuitions, my wife is quite able to cope with any situation." He does not hesitate to say that, though he is a noncomformist in certain areas of life and even in his art, "I'm very middle class, very square, in my own marriage and my own family life. I don't want to have far-out children and a far-out marriage." Of the three Roces children, Mia most actively shares her father's interest in art. Not too long ago, father and daughter enjoyed equal billing in a two-person exhibition of their paintings.

Now that he is "closer to becoming a gentleman of leisure," as he calls this interlude between one full-time job and the next, he has become "a little more active" in painting. He still keeps company with the Saturday Group of artists, so called because they meet every Saturday at Taza de Oro for coffee and small talk, and goes on sketching trips with Cesar Legaspi and other outdoor watercolorists on Thursdays. He is also readying a one-man show for next month. While he values stimulating company, he also likes being alone — reading, researching or maybe feeding the pet fish he keeps in the pond at his home. Lately, though, he has started to relish the time he spends with his children, as a parent who realizes they won't be young and his forever.

An avid poker player until his friends started playing more for the money than for the fun of it, he is a great believer in luck as a major factor in life and has never found it to his advantage to plan ahead. "Eighty percent of my life has been things I did not foresee." If he has to speak at all of an ultimate goal, he puts it vaguely: "To be able to write and to be able to paint." And, not to forget, "I'd like to be an authentic person."

Goodman
February 1976

Alfredo R. Roces has been living with his family in Australia since the early Eighties. He edited GEO Magazine *for many years. He comes to Manila to mount one-man shows and has produced a number of books, the latest of which is about the artist Ang Kiu Kok. He was editorial consultant to* The Philippines: A Journey Through the Archipelago.

Lolita Rodriguez
A Real Winner

"Ice" is how some quarters in the Philippine movie industry describe the tall, elegant woman who, for the 20-plus years she has been in the business, has refused to be part of its sham and its glitter, preferring to be part only of its beauty and giving only her best to this art that she loves with a passion. "Ice" she must surely be to those in the industry who live by the rules of the game, and what rules they are, when one has to suffer the banalities of *Tito* Joe and *Ate* Luds and *Kuya* Nards and every little movie reporter who wants to milk one's privacy dry; when the movie fan feels that, in exchange for her undying devotion she is entitled to dictate how one should live one's life; when one's success has to be equated with the loss of one's dignity.

I knew her reputation — the Philippines' Greta Garbo, they also call her — and was apprehensive about the assignment, yet intrigued by the woman who is the country's best in her profession but also, for someone of her stature, its least known. Two years ago, she quietly left for the United States, but early in January just as quietly came back, to appear in PETA's revival of *Larawan*, the Tagalog translation of Nick Joaquin's *Portrait of the Artist as Filipino*, and in a Lino Brocka movie for Regal Films. At the press conference called by Regal Films to announce her homecoming, I had to take a second look, for I had expected to see someone who looked like a movie star, fully made up, colorfully attired, you know the sort. That was how little I knew of her. For there she was, exuding casual American chic in a beige sweater blouse and a brown skirt, looking tanned and youngish, speaking in soft tones to the reporters who sat with her, smiling often, being awfully nice. There were no screaming fans, no *alalay* in sight, just this lovely, poised woman. She was no movie star.

LOLITA RODRIGUEZ

"But I've never been a movie star, have never felt like one," she is saying now as she sips coffee in the living room of the tiny apartment her friend Lino Brocka found for her. It is a transient's flat furnished with a transient's meager needs. On the kitchen shelf are a bottle of Sue Bee Honey, a can of FITA biscuits, several cans of Alaska milk, a small can of Baguio oil, a tiny can of Queensland butter, a bottle of Nescafe. On the dish rack, a solitary plate, two glasses, two saucers, two cups. On the lamp table in the living room lies a copy of Liv Ullmann's bestseller, *Changing*, a going-away gift for Lolita from some friends in the States. A suitcase stands under the dresser in the bedroom.

She is looking relaxed and slim in a loose flowery blouse and white pants, the fragrance of Diane Von Furstenberg's Tatiana enveloping her. "A gift from my children," she says, beaming.

She laughs at mention of her Greta Garbo image. "Maybe the mystery is good," she says. "I find people who are a little mysterious very interesting. People keep asking why don't I open up, but I didn't really think I want to do this, I want to do that. I probably had it in me all the time but didn't realize it."

"I am," she continues, "a very aloof person. When I'm relaxed with someone, I'm not so aloof. When I'm not relaxed, I put a line and make them feel that line. It's wrong to judge a person but when you don't feel anything, you don't, and you can't change that, no matter how broad-minded you are. It's human nature, I guess. I manage to be nice to people, not all the time, but I try. It doesn't take too much to be nice. But if there is something I don't like I don't have to say anything. People can feel and see it. Maybe that's why they say I'm aloof. But people who know me well don't say I'm aloof; they say I'm reserved. I don't know. They say I'm weird."

No, Lolita Rodriguez is not weird. She just had enough good sense to decide, years ago, that if she was to remain sane in a highly competitive and fickle business, she had to draw a line between her private life and what her public was entitled to know. "Lolita's public image," says Lino Brocka, "is of a very rational, very hard woman. *Laging matatag daw.* Well, she is. But when you get to know her, she is very gentle, very warm, very soft-spoken."

Brocka, Lolita's friend these past 19 years, recalls the advice she gave him when he was new in the industry. "She said, 'when I have to shoot, I shoot, but when I get home I close the door and what is behind that door is my life.' *Sabi niya,* how tragic *naman na ang ikinabubuhay mo ay ang pagaartista, sa tunay na buhay ay artista ka pa rin.*"

It would be hypocrisy to claim that Lolita Rodriguez, in all her years as an actress, never for a moment revelled in the glamour of it. She did. "For a while," she admits, "when you've just started, you enjoy it." But, as she once told a friend of hers, she experienced an awakening when she was 28, in her tenth year in the game, and she is grateful for that. Very few in show business are as lucky. "There is," says Brocka, "a very thin line between illusion and reality so that sometimes movie stars tend to believe that what they are doing on the screen is real."

Dr. Lourdes V. Lapuz, a psychologist, puts it another way: "There is something about a constant fishbowl existence that can make a person just drown. It's very difficult to be always 'on'. You begin to feel fakey, phony, sometimes, because you have to fulfill roles not only in reel but also in real life, and you begin to wonder who is the real person underneath all of this."

WHAT AMAZES IS that Lolita Rodriguez' good sense is largely self-taught. She quit school in her teens because her American father had died and her mother was pushing the boys among her nine children. Lolita Clark, American mestiza, was too *morena* by the cinematic standards of the day, but in her neighborhood lived a man who encouraged her childhood fantasies.

Juan Silos, who was a musical director for Sampaguita Pictures, was her neighbor in Sampaloc and he had lived out the wartime years rehearsing dramatic shows in his home with his friends. The little Clark girl used to visit the Silos house just to watch those rehearsals. "I remember the late Maria Cristina was the leading lady," she says. "I would emote in one corner on my own, crying when she cried, laughing when she did." Silos knew she wanted to act, in fact always asked her whether she wanted to be in the movies. Her answer was always a determined yes.

But it was not Silos who helped her break into the movies. It was Felix Avellana who took her not to Sampaguita, but to LVN, where his brother Lamberto was directing a movie that starred Mila del Sol and Jaime de la Rosa. Lolita recalls, "They gave me a simple screen test. I just had to sit down and say my name. They asked me to smile, look to my left, look to my right, things like that." She never heard from LVN after that, perhaps because, she surmises, she did not have the porcelain skin prescribed for film goddesses of that period.

Not long afterward, Silos took her to Sampaguita for a different kind of screen test. Tony Cayado and Linda Estrella were doing a film then and were preparing for an emotional scene. Lolita was handed the actress's script and told to memorize her lines. The scene with Cayado called for her to cry — "I thought I would die" — and all those times when, as a little girl, she had watched Maria Cristina and then retreated to her little corner of the Silos house to do her own private crying, paid off.

As far as acting was concerned, she had made it. But she was told that she did not photograph well. It was the heavy screen makeup which, until today, does not suit her. Four screen tests later, after each of which she would be assigned "extra" roles ("Nobody put makeup on the extras so I looked all right"), Dr. Perez had a Sampaguita cameraman photograph her from all possible angles. "After that, he just called me and asked if I'd like to sign a contract. I did, with no permission from my mother. I said, My God, this is what I want to do, I'll do it."

She was 18, not too young by the standards of Alma Moreno and Lorna Tolentino, but certainly young enough to lose her balance. Today, looking forward to her forty-fourth birthday, she muses, "To be exposed to a world like that is gratifying. If I had started on my own, it would have been very hard. But I was with Sampaguita and like everyone else there, I was guided and trained. Otherwise, I'd probably be lost."

She became a star in *Jack and Jill*, and her leading man was Rogelio de la Rosa, the idol of her childhood. She was so flustered she could not do anything on the first day of shooting. "I couldn't memorize my lines, I couldn't even move, so we just spent the day getting acquainted." De La Rosa was, she remembers, very nice, and made her feel he had known her for years. They are still good friends, and when De La Rosa came home from his diplomatic post in Europe the other year for the LVN celebration of Doña Sisang's birth centennial, it was only Lolita Rodriguez whose presence, outside of the LVN family of stars, he requested at a reunion in his honor.

She never developed a star complex. While filming *Jack and Jill*, she would bike all the way from her friend's house in Pasay to the Luneta. Her studio, had it known, would have been dismayed. She remembers, however, being fined by the studio for waterskiing in Parañaque until her skin became too dark for Mrs. Nene Vera-Perez' taste. "*Sabi ni Mrs. Perez,*" Lolita recalls, "*ang kulay kong naisusuot lang,* white. *Hirap na hirap na raw siyang pumili ng damit para sa akin.* Now, if I were conscious of being a movie star, I wouldn't have done that."

There was time enough to be spent with her fans, who were at that time a relatively well-mannered lot. They would come to her house on Sunday afternoons and she would always make herself available, even for their picnics and balls and fund-raising affairs. "They weren't just screaming all over the place," she says. "They formed useful organizations." And even when her star shown brightest, all she had by way of an *alalay* was a maid to carry her makeup box and costumes. Sometimes she even dispensed with such assistance. "I could work better when I was alone on the set because I would worry about the person who was with me. She might be bored or hungry or whatever. It bothered me so."

ALMOST AS SOON as Lolita Rodriguez signed a contract with Sampaguita, she told herself, "I cannot start this way and still be here after 20 years." She wanted badly to improve her craft. Tackling a variety of roles — action, comedy and drama — she managed to evade being typecast. She could play the suffering heroine or the other woman with equal ease.

Early on she discovered that drama does not mean hysterics. "So many people," she says, "have the notion that if it's a dramatic movie your tears have to fall. I've always been against that. I believe the inner thing is always stronger than the outward thing. It's very easy to get hysterical, very easy, but to be restrained and yet project everything you're feeling to the audience is the challenge. I like to do dramatic scenes without shedding a tear, and yet make my audience cry."

Today, with two FAMAS awards as best actress to her name (for her roles in *Gilda* and *Tinimbang Ka Nguni't Kulang*), she still confesses to feeling drained after every movie. "I feel everything inside me when I'm shooting. That's why I have to drink coffee. It relaxes me. In the beginning I used to feel terribly drained. But one gets used to it. I still feel drained but I get over it a little faster."

Brocka, who has gone on record as saying that Lolita Rodriguez is his favorite actress, explains the lady's unique talent. "When it comes to restraint in acting," he says, "Lolita knows how to quantify emotions. She has not only intelligence, but also depth as a person." She is, according to Brocka, "very *metikulosa*, very technique-oriented." While other stars nonchalantly report to the set, oftentimes hours late, and simply wait for the director's cue, Lolita makes it her business to come on time, to know what will go into every scene and whether the crew is ready for it. Brocka should know. He was making *Tinimbang*, he says, and "we were rehearsing. Then, when we were starting to shoot, something went wrong with the lights. Lolita was in the middle of a scene and she stopped. She didn't say anything, and then she looked at everybody and said, very deliberately, '*Punyeta!*' Then she stood in the center, told the men to check everything, and said, '*Baka gusto ninyo kayo ang tumayo dito.*' Her point was it was a difficult scene and people were taking it for granted. She's very professional. That's why a lot of people enjoy working with her. She's the sort of actress who gives you something to react to."

She explains the way she portrayed Kuala, the woman driven to insanity in *Tinimbang*: "Well, hers was a true story. I spoke to a lot of people about her. My best guide was that she was crazy. Now, how was I going to portray this crazy woman? There are so many ways of being crazy. I kept reading the script until a picture came out, until it was clear to me. Kuala had her insane moments and her sane moments. So you don't come up with a plain crazy woman who is dreaming and doing atrocious things all over the place. I thought it had to be some kind of inner craziness and that's how I portrayed her."

Sampaguita kept Lolita under contract for 12 years, eight of them on an exclusive basis. She is proud of practically every one of those years. "The first years," she sums them up, "were good because I was just starting. Then, when I was able to take off, it was also a good year. But you want to go higher, like the year I made *Gilda*. Once you're up there, you want to maintain that position, and not only maintain it because so many others have done that, but do so in a very respectable manner. You have to win respect not only for your talent but for yourself as a person."

Both forms of recognition are hers now, of course. On that point there is no debate. Lolita Rodriguez is the country's premier actress. She knows that, and while she is modest about the distinction, she is not falsely so. "When foreigners come and ask for an actress's name and they give my name right away, then you know you made it." What gives her particular pleasure is knowing that the achievement has been won without benefit of formal schooling, but through sheer on-the-job persistence. "It gives me," she says, "a nice feeling to know that without any training, what I'm doing is right. It gives me a very good feeling."

The same self-confidence makes her disdainful of flattery and unimpressed by status and power. A male movie reporter made the mistake of cooing, while walking alongside her once, "*Ay, ang ganda-ganda talaga ni Lolita Rodriguez!*" She stopped in her tracks, waved an arm at him, said, "*Diyan ka lang,*" and went on her way. Ten years ago, while rehearsing for *Larawan* at Raha Sulayman Theatre in Fort Santiago, she and the rest of the cast were visited by Nick Joaquin himself. Lolita was sitting casually in a chair, recalls Lino Brocka, while Joaquin proceeded to show her how he wanted Paula, the character she was playing, to stir the native chocolate in one scene. He rambled on, endlessly it seemed, about how he wanted the rest of the play to be done. Still sitting in her chair, puffing away at a Marlboro, she told Cecile Guidote who was directing the play, "*Palayasin mo iyan.*" Cecile was distressed; how could anyone do that to Nick Joaquin? "*Wala akong pakialam,*" Lolita replied, at the same time threatening to walk out if Joaquin did not. She got her wish, and a compliment from the playwright to boot. "That's my Paula," he was reported to have said.

For the repeat performance of *Larawan* this month, Lolita is playing Candida to Charito Solis's Paula. She has already warned Joaquin that she will play the role differently. "All right," said Joaquin who has become a Lolita Rodriguez fan, "as long as it is honest."

"*Pag hindi niya gusto,*" Lino Brocka warns, "*dederetsuhin ka niya.* She's very nice, very diplomatic about it, but everybody knows when she's mad."

Brocka has been in show business long enough to form valid perceptions of the star system. He is only too aware that in the movie world, where success is measured in terms of the number of movies made and the price a star commands, actresses like Lolita Rodriguez and Hilda Koronel are not in the running. But Brocka disagrees. "They say, si Lolita, si Hilda, *walang pelikula, walang pera,* victims *daw ng* star system. *Sabi ko, mali,* those are the winners. When Hilda or Lolita wants to say *punyeta,* they go right ahead, they tell you."

Lolita Rodriguez is the example Brocka cites to people like Bembol Roco and Phillip Salvador, both of whom he discovered. "I try to prepare them for what is to come because what is to come is quite disastrous. If you don't watch out, boy, it will eat you up and destroy you. So I say, look, you can't beat the system, I know I can't. But what you can do is make the system bow to you, acknowledge you when you come in. Like when Lolita Rodriguez walks in there are no screaming fans but there's a hush and people turn around and whisper, 'That's Lolita Rodriguez.' That's what you can make the system do. I've seen that. At a premiere night when everybody is screaming, there's a hush when Lolita comes in. She never allows herself to be kissed, but she's very nice."

Brocka has a term for this aura that pervades Lolita Rodriguez. "I call it pizzazz," he says, "and I don't mean it in the vulgar sense. I mean it in the sense that she fills a place with her presence."

Her two-year absence from the screen has not dissipated the magic of her name. It is very much missed, specially during this period of mediocrity and unabashed vulgarity. Her comeback, if only for one picture, sharpens the contrast between her and the present crop of young bodies, for that is all the others are. She had been making fewer films in the more recent past, averaging two a year, sometimes only one. She wanted it that way, believing that if she made one or two that were good, she would be satisfied as an actress. "People say you need exposure; too much is bad, so is too little. It really depends on what you can do. If you can give something that people will remember for the rest of the year, it's okay."

TWO YEARS AGO, Lolita finally made the move she had been mulling since 1970. She had always wanted to live in the United States, but she was biding her time, waiting until her children were all grown. The move was as much for herself as for them. For herself, because "I wanted to live a different life. I just wanted to be one of the crowd, be free, work like an ordinary person and enjoy myself." For her children, because "I want them to be independent" while also wanting for them a traditional Filipino upbringing.

They are all grown now — Birdie, Bogey and Par, her three children by former actor Eddie Arenas, all nicknamed after terms commonly used in the sport that had first brought their parents together. The marriage is a no-no subject even today, 16 years after it ended. Lolita sits back in her chair and looks up at the ceiling, saying wistfully, when asked how long her marriage lasted, "Eight years, and we've been separated for 16 — that's twice as many years as we were together." I cannot ignore the pain in that statement, for surely Lolita Rodriguez has known anguish and loneliness. She isn't saying so, only that when there are painful moments in her life, "I try to solve them if I can, but things I cannot solve, I don't try, I try to ignore. I keep most painful things to myself, that's the way I am. As the years pass you probably become an expert and it's not difficult anymore. When you're younger, everything is painful anyway. But I always manage to be in control, which is probably why it's so easy for me to be restrained."

I am tempted to press, to ask what went wrong, but the line has been drawn, and so I ask the next question: Was it very difficult being a single parent? "In the beginning," she says softly, "yes. After a while you get used to it. The thing I found a little difficult was being a single parent to a boy who was growing up. You have to be very firm and prove that you're strong so he will look up to you." She has done pretty well by them. Birdie, a child study graduate of Maryknoll in Quezon City, is 23 and soon to be a bride. Bogey, the only son, is almost 21 and in the Navy in Oakland, California. He has given his mother her first grandchild, a two-year-old girl. Par, Lolita's youngest who, Lino Brocka swears, is a Jean Peters look-alike, is graduating from high school in the U.S. and is set to enroll in a filmmaking course.

"My children," Lolita says, "are three different individuals. In certain things I have a rule for everyone, but as far as their way of thinking and emotional makeup are concerned, they have to be treated as individuals. It is so interesting to watch them and see them develop into maturity. I think people are so lucky to experience their children."

With her children she maintains a "very close" relationship. "We talk about anything at all. Even with my son, I can talk about anything, even sex. *Nagdidisco sila, nauuna pa ako sa* dancefloor. Whatever they enjoy, I do too. Some people are 50 and feel like 60. *Ako*, I feel I'm a teenager."

In Los Angeles, she is an employee at Lyons United Parts, Inc., an automotive parts distributor where she says she handles everything in the mailing department. The setup is "very good and comfortable, there are no intrigues." Never having had a star complex, she found it easy to adjust to office routine and anonymity. It was only when she asked for a leave that her boss found out who and what she was in the Philippines, and even then he would not believe her. "He said I didn't look like a movie star."

She has, she says, grown tremendously since she left Manila. "I know how to work. Here, when I had no *labandera*, I washed, I ironed. I can cook, I can chop wood with an ax *pa*. I can do anything. My frustration is to make my own furniture. I want my children to learn that, *para kung marunong ka, tapos* you have to do it, *hindi ka nahihirapan, pati loob mo hindi nahihirapan*. But if you don't know, *tapos napipilitan kang gumawa, ang bigat*.

"I've grown so much, I'm more tolerant now. My outlook, my attitudes, they're different now. I could be given just a small clip for my hair and it excites me so much. A little thing can excite me, make me happy."

Acting remains an obsession with her. She would like to make it in Hollywood or on Broadway, perhaps when Par has settled down. "When my children are all married," she says, smiling, "when they have their own lives, then I don't care if I'm 60 years old, I'll be there. I always tell my children it's never too late to embark on something new." There are other plans for the time when she will be free to think of herself: a trip to London and, perhaps, involvement in British theatre; a book like Liv Ullman's *Changing*, that will be "very simple, very honest"; an occasional film in Manila, when the role is right.

Maybe, too, a new life. "A woman," she says, "will always need a man." Her requirements are formidable: responsibility, maturity, kindness, gentleness, strength, everything, she says, that is supposed to be in a man. "He's almost there," she volunteers, and I detect a radiance in her eyes that was not there earlier, "but there is nothing solid at the moment." I surmise the person she is speaking of fits the description she has given as coming closest to the ideal: "He has to be a very, very lovely person inside, someone I can relate to and feel very comfortable with, and with whom I can enjoy things we have in common. This time it has to be like that."

This time, I hope she makes it. Happiness is the least we can wish her who has given us so much of that, and more.

Celebrity
February 15, 1979

Lolita Rodriguez lives on a farm in California with her American husband. Her friends here say she has found happiness after her disappointments with the movie industry which she chose to keep to herself. Five years ago, shortly after her friend Lino Brocka died, she came home for a visit. Earlier, in mid-1984, she came to do the film Paradise Inn, *directed by Celso Ad. Castillo. She was nominated for her role as an ex-prostitute in the movie, but the award for best actress went instead to Vivian Velez, the film's producer, who played her daughter.*

If Vilma Comes, Can Edgar Be Far Behind?

In the colorful world of the Filipino movie fan, circa 1971, the ideological lines (with all due respect to the radicals and the moderates in the movement) are sharply drawn. One is either for Nora Aunor or for Vilma Santos. One cannot like both and be worthy of the name "movie fan." In fact, there are no fans in the case of Nora and Vilma; there are only fanatics.

Nora, her loyal subjects maintain, has a far better singing voice than Vilma. That, counters the Santos camp, is because Vilma is primarily an actress and only incidentally a singer. And Vilma of the doll-like face is definitely the prettier of the two, her fanatics boast. There, we think, the debate should end.

The day we interviewed Nora Aunor we swore to ourself we would never again do a story on a movie star. The ordeal of waiting for hours and finally getting a mere 30 minutes of the Superstar's time was just too much for our nerves. Never again, we vowed. Those were famous last words.

The assignment was to interview Vilma Santos for a cover story. We were told that we could catch her one Saturday morning at an Antipolo resort where she was shooting *Wonderful World of Music* for Tagalog Ilang-Ilang. Her director was there, all right, and so was Snooky, too self-conscious and too small for her age. But Vilma was still in Cabanatuan, and so was Edgar.

The following Wednesday she was scheduled to start filming for another Tagalog Ilang-Ilang picture, *Young Lovers*. With a title like that, we thought, the movie couldn't be anything but a further buildup of the Edgar-Vilma love team. But who wants a story when you can have your fill of Vilma and Edgar exchanging sweet words and glances?

VILMA SANTOS

We were at this house in Quezon City, site of the first day of shooting, at nine in the morning. The entire cast and crew were there, except for the leading lady and her leading man. When they arrived an hour and a half later, the place seemed to come alive. The young lovers (should the word be enclosed in quotation marks?) were chaperoned by Mrs. Santos, pretty and amply proportioned.

We were relieved to see none of the burly tomboys who smothered Nora. It was Edgar Mortiz, with his height and size, who looked more like Vilma's bodyguard. If he were slim and shorter, he could pass for her shadow. Yet it is difficult to imagine him in the role of bodyguard; he is what older folk would describe as *mukhang musmos pa*. Edgar Mortiz is, in fact, younger than Vilma Santos who, at 17, is no giggly teenager. She is a woman and she knows it.

"A LOT of people tell me that I am very mature for my age," she says at the start of the interview. "I feel it myself. I like to think that I have the mind of a 23-year-old woman." She speaks with unusual poise and self-confidence, a self-assurance which must explain why she strikes some people as *suplada*.

Vilma had little time to be a child. When she was nine and a student at St. Mary's Academy in Manila, an uncle who was a cameraman at Sampaguita introduced her to Dr. Jose Perez. Not long afterward, Rosa Vilma Santos made her first film, *Trudis Liit*, where she played the title role. Shooting schedules were arranged so as not to conflict with her studies: she attended school in the morning, reported to the set in the afternoon. More pictures for Sampaguita followed, including two on the life of Ferdinand Marcos, in which she was cast as Imee.

When the time came for Vilma to choose between school and a film career, she readily chose the latter. "We study so we can get a job later, *hindi ba?* Well, I have a job already." When she does decide to resume her studies (she was in fourth year high when she quit), she wants to go into fine arts.

Right now, however, her thoughts are on her career and, if we are to believe her studio's drumbeaters, Edgar. Is he or isn't he?

That is as intriguing a question to their fanatics as Imelda Marcos's political ambition is to newspaper columnists. The love team of Vilma and Edgar has been going strong for two years now. Whether on TV's *Sensations* and *Edgar Loves Vilma* or on radio's "Hot Line 1250 with Edgar and Vilma" or in advertising gimmicks, the latest of which is a birthday party with Edgar and Vilma, the team-up has proved to be a hit. They are, in addition, neighbors somewhere in Quezon City.

Doesn't she get tired of being paired with him? "Of course not," she says petulantly. Whether their apparent fondness for each other is the real thing or just plain acting is hard to tell. When not holding hands, which is most of the time, they have their arms around each other. "I'm not really a singer," Vilma admits, "but Edgar is teaching me how to sing."

Love teams come and go, but that is the least of Vilma's worries. Show business is her world. She wants to stay in it for as long as she can. "*Sana magtagal ako*," she says.

Even without her Edgar?

Asia-Philippines Leader
July 9, 1971

Vilma Santos at 45 has made a midlife career shift. From being the Star for all Seasons, enduring box office queen, awardwinning actress and successful TV star, she plunged into politics following her marriage to Ralph Recto in 1994. The following year, Recto won a congressional seat representing Batangas largely on the basis of his marriage to the star. In 1998 Vilma herself ran for mayor in Lipa City and won a landslide victory. Unlike other showbiz personalities turned politicians, Vilma prepared for her new role by studying: she enrolled, along with 20 of her staff, in a crash course at the U.P. College of Public Administration where teachers praised her eagerness to learn. She has already announced that she has no further political ambitions. Before her marriage to the much younger Recto, she had well publicized affairs with several men, notably the former

Sampaguita matinee idol Romeo Vasquez, and a short-lived marriage to Edu Manzano, an actor and now vice mayor of Makati City. She has two sons: 16-year-old Lucky by Manzano and two-year-old Christian by Recto.

Edgar Mortiz, on the other hand, is now a television director with a family of his own.

JOY AND PIO DE CASTRO
Not Your Usual Love Story

It looks – and feels – very much like a house in transition, all three stories of it on this narrow stretch of road called Victory. Boxes stand in one's way in the living room and the sala set has been stripped of its covers. The dining table is bare. There is a tentativeness in the air, even a sadness broken only by the yelping of a frisky white Pomeranian named Nikki.

"This house was beautiful when it was a living thing," Nikki's mistress says softly.

So it must have been. The man of the house threw parties twice or thrice a week. He liked having exciting, interesting people around him and he was always the perfect host, his wife remembers. On the feast of St. John the Baptist, the town's patron saint, the open-house party would last from dusk to dawn.

But the party's over in the house on Victory Street. The man of the house lies still on a hospital bed on the third floor, in what resembles a hospital room — with a suction machine, a stand-by oxygen tank, bottles of medicine on a side table, nurses round the clock. He has been that way since October 1993 when he suffered a stroke, his third in six years.

JOY SOLER de Castro calls herself a widow with a living husband. She is 44, a smart, attractive and vibrant woman who made waves as a stage actress and for 19 years was an officer at the Department of Tourism.

She was in Fort Santiago in the early Seventies rehearsing for a play with the fledgling Philippine Educational Theatre Association

JOY SOLER de CASTRO

(PETA), when Pio de Castro literally walked into her life. He strode in, looking very casual and confident in Levi's, T-shirt and sneakers, and went up to PETA founder and director Cecile Guidote. They were old friends, it turned out, who had not seen each other since the young man returned from studies in Michigan, USA, where he majored in film.

Every evening after that, Pio would drop by the Fort after work hours at Image Films. He liked the theatre, too, and after a week Cecile cooked up an acting project for him, an off-off-Broadway play called *The Last Sweet Days of Isaac*. His leading lady was to be Joy, who had just graduated (cum laude, communication arts) from St. Paul College Manila. Despite her sheltered upbringing, she consented to appear in one scene wearing only a bra and a slip while Pio wore only briefs. Together they shocked their audiences.

They became friends while doing the play. She was totally taken by him. "He was one big, huge brain. There were no limits to the way he could think. He would talk about philosophical things, never mundane things, and there was no idle talk for him. But he was not stiff nor distant. He was a very open spirit and he had a rich, full voice. And a laugh that was so crisp. There was no mean bone in his body. He liked women, was so comfortable with them. And he was nice even with gays. He thoroughly enjoyed them and had such respect for them."

Pio was not her first boyfriend but it was he, a bohemian who disdained rules and convention, who taught her about being a woman. "I guess I grew up with him," Joy says.

When they decided to marry in 1978 after being friends for almost eight years, there were no principal sponsors, no one gave the bride away (she and Pio walked into the chapel arm in arm), and they wrote their own vows, promising each other freedom: "Marriage was not going to restrict what we could become."

"I didn't want a career," says Joy, who was already at the Department of Tourism then. "All I wanted to be was a mistress. I was going to be a servile woman to a man."

But Pio believed otherwise. He didn't want her to be his appendage. His philosophy, as far as she was concerned, Joy says, was that she had to grow, to use her talents, to have her own name.

He himself was kept busy directing commercials for television — he would come home at two in the morning and be off again four hours later. There was hardly time for them to talk. In fact, she says, he stopped talking to her the way he used to do before they were married. She started wishing they had stayed just friends. "We were happy and yet I was always lonely." She never told anyone, however. Their friends all thought they were a perfect couple.

She was so eager to hear him in conversation that when friends and associates of his would come around for meetings or just plain talk, she would serve them herself just so she could hang around them.

Her father had taught her to be tough, never to cry. Her mother had taught her never to burden her husband with problems. Somewhere along the way she had also been told never to put her man in any dilemma.

"It was a real pain, that I lived with this man for so long and he never talked to me. Everybody, even the women, said he was such a listener. It made me so angry. I reached a point where I said that if I was just going to be so lonely we could split up and still be the best of friends. I was so confident we could go back to where we started."

THAT WAS in 1985. Soon enough Joy accepted a job in Singapore that would take her away for two years. She did not even ask him if he wanted to go with her. She needed the breathing space that Singapore offered. The arrangement seemed to suit both of them: he would visit her and she would fly to Manila to see him.

She was in Singapore when Pio had his first stroke, which paralyzed the left side of his body but fortunately spared his left brain. They should have seen it coming — his father had died after a stroke, as had one brother and an uncle. The doctors did not give Pio much of a chance, but he proved them wrong. Although he was in the hospital for six months, he was able to walk again, aided by a cane, after a year in a wheelchair. He resumed writing film critiques and teaching at the University of the Philippines and Ateneo. He was even able to go back to directing, though not as vigorously as before.

Their friends teased Joy that she was the only one they knew who gained weight while tending to a sick person. She told them she was happy caring for him, and she meant it. It was her way of communicating with Pio.

When he recovered, she found that their relationship had not improved. He still would not talk to her. Every time she started a conversation with him, his blood pressure would rise. She tried to talk with him about money, but "I didn't get all the answers either." She did not know how much money he earned and where it was, or whether he was insured. They did not have a joint bank account.

The second stroke hit Pio in January 1993. He was having dinner at a restaurant with some theatre people when he felt his body going numb. He walked himself to his car and instructed his driver to take him to Manila Doctors Hospital.

Pio's first words to Joy when she arrived at the hospital were "I'm sorry, I'm sick again." This time she was angry. "I felt he had it coming. He wasn't taking care of himself. *Nadamay ako.*"

That stroke affected Pio's left brain. His speech became slurred. But again he recovered. Within a month after going home, he was able to climb the stairs and bathe himself. He was also able to write again, although he tended to repeat himself.

In May that year Joy organized a bash at the Coconut Palace to celebrate Pio's fiftieth birthday. She asked guests to come as Filipino characters. Pio came as a *barong*-ed Apolinario Mabini in a wheelchair.

Just five months later, on October 17, 1993, Pio had his third stroke while he was asleep. It was a Sunday and Joy had gone to church. She returned home to find the gate and the front door open and people milling outside and inside the house.

Her first reaction was, "Oh no, we're going back to the hospital. Life is going to change again. And then the expenses."

Then the thought hit her — this was the way life would be for them. Pio was never going to get well.

The relay system in his brain had been so badly damaged that his doctors said he would never again be the brilliant man that he was. The biggest casualty was his lungs. Joy found out he had been smoking behind her back even after the second stroke, and she felt cheated — and angry with him for being "a selfish man."

One night in early December, as she prepared to take him home after two and a half months in hospital, she realized that what she was taking home was "a shell of a man," the child she never had. She who had been taught not to cry, who could not shed tears even after her father was murdered, now cried as she had never cried before.

She remembers that day well because it was the day she turned herself around. When her eyes ran out of tears, and her best friends had prayed over her, she felt a tremendous sense of relief, of a burden being lifted from her. "I accepted. And I finally forgave him. I wasn't angry anymore." It was, she recalls, as though God wanted to clean her up because she was taking home a very sick husband who needed her to be whole.

PIO DE CASTRO, acclaimed film and commercial director (his *Soltero* is a widely praised movie and his TV commercials are said to be among the best in the industry), eminent film critic (he was a co-founder of the Manunuri ng Pelikulang Pilipino), consummate teacher and bon vivant, lives in a room that Joy has enlivened with wallpaper plastered with photographs and greeting cards and letters from friends. He is fed by tube. Although his blood pressure has stabilized and his temperature is less erratic, he requires close monitoring.

Joy, who occupies the room next to his, goes in to see him as soon as she wakes up in the morning and looks in on him several times during the day. "He is not comatose," she starts to explain. "Sometimes I say, 'Pangga, 1+1,' and he shows me two fingers. There is a level of understanding but he cannot communicate back. Sometimes I sense that he is very sad. I worry about that. I never tell him when we have a problem, that funds may be running out sometimes. I pretend that everything is all right."

Never one who had to work for income or to worry about money, she now has to work to pay for the 24-hour nurses, the special food and regulated environment that Pio requires, the doctors, the medicines. Since leaving DOT, she has set up an events organizing company that is based right in her home. When she has to go out of town on business, she leaves detailed instructions with the nurses and the househelp. Although prepared for the worst scenario, she worries that she might not be around if and when Pio goes.

While she feels herself a widow, she is not quite ready to be one. She frets that she still has Pio's papers to put in order, his collection of rare books on film to donate to Ateneo's communication arts department (he has an astounding collection of books, video tapes, *Classics Illustrated*, *Playboy* and *Hustler* magazines, even *Hiwaga* and *Pilipino komiks*).

The only thing Joy would like to keep of Pio's is a series of postcards he sent her every day for three weeks in 1974 when he went around Southeast Asia for a documentary. It is, she says, her "most priceless possession of Pio because he never did any romantic thing ever again."

Since Pio's last stroke she has been merely going through the days, not thinking too much. But at night she muses on her life and in her mind grapples with questions — from the practical (How low, how far would I beg? How would Pio feel if he knew I was accepting money from other people?) to the moral (Will I allow myself to be married while my husband is alive? I'm young, I'm very vulnerable when I'm lonely. But can I take care of another man? Or will I insist that somebody now take care of me because I am tired?).

Above all, this moral dilemma: If he has another stroke, how far will I go? How do I know when it is time to let him go? And whom is she sparing when it is time to pull the plug — him or herself? Pio had once told her he didn't want to be a vegetable; he had seen that in his mother just before she died.

People inevitably ask Joy how she keeps herself sane. She tells them she has a supportive family and many best friends, all of them prayerful. They have helped her to refine a concept of faith that had always been there but had not been nurtured. Having learned to submit herself to God's will, she has also learned to be more forgiving of those at the DOT who she says treated her unfairly and made her life there miserable.

And she has learned to love Pio again.

"For a while, I thought I didn't love him because I was so angry with him after his third stroke. I felt I was an unwilling victim. But I never doubted that he really loved me. I just wished he loved me another way. Now I care for him without any anger. So I am grateful for this borrowed time. I have come to accept that what loving is really all about is you take the person for what he is, not what you perceived him to be. That, in fairness to him, is what he has done for me. He took me for what I am."

There is regret for the years that she and Pio have lost. They were so rarely alone together and vacations were few and far between.

The future she doesn't even want to think about. But in her newfound calm she can joke that her perception of her ideal man has changed: *"Hindi na importanteng mautak; kahit bobo, basta kinakausap ako."*

Inside a coffee shop she sees an elderly couple holding hands. "I wonder if I'll ever have that," she says, cupping her face with her hands. "If I were to grow old, I will need somebody who will hold my hand."

Sunday Inquirer Magazine
February 12, 1995

Joy Soler de Castro juggles her time between caring for Pio and running Events Plus, an event management and organization company. Almost five years after Pio's worst stroke, she says, his mental alertness has improved, making it possible for them to interact more. But he is becoming "progressively thinner despite the continuing nutritional supplements to his regular feedings." Joy also says Pio is now able to inject emotive texture to his grunts and 'sound effects.' When his close friend, the film director Ishmael Bernal, died in 1996, he shed tears when Joy broke the news to him. A poster of Mexican telenovela star Thalia hangs in his room, Pio having become a fan of hers while watching her popular drama series **Mari Mar.**

Susie Winternitz Returns to Nature

Susie Winternitz walks out of her bedroom with brisk, purposeful strides, so like the old Belgian nuns of one's girlhood. As she walks, she struggles with the clasp of a necklace, from which dangle Snoopy and the words "World's greatest grandmother." It is a title she has been wearing proudly for two years now, as grandmother to a little boy who calls her "Bamboo" because it was the first word he ever uttered, perhaps because he saw so much of it in his grandmother's home.

What profound truth the child in his innocence has perceived! But then he might as well also call her Rattan or Buri or Coconut, for Susie Winternitz has all of those in her home, too. In fact, for the past 43 years, she has been collecting bamboo, dried grass and leaves, various parts of the coconut, rattan, *buri*, mango seeds, *tingting*, *gugo*, fish scales and other materials that less imaginative mortals so thoughtlessly discard. And out of this "garbage" she has created things of delicate, fascinating beauty.

The bungalow she is renting in Quezon City is rich with these materials and products of her creative hands, plus discoveries she has made on her many trips around the Philippines. The living room furniture is bamboo: short squat bamboo storage boxes which used to fit under the bamboo sofa and now do equally well as a coffee table. Atop this table are clay *bibingka* dishes from Vigan; they come in various sizes, indicating the number of *bibingka* each can hold. Also on the table, amid newspapers and magazines from Ms. Winternitz's native Austria, is a clay container for chicken feed. The clay pieces, including her collection of clay jars for different purposes, she discovered on sorties to public markets. "I love to go to market," she enthuses. "It's the first thing I ask to see

SUSIE WINTERNITZ

when I go to the province." Among the rarer pieces in her collection of clay jars and pots is a native double boiler from Calbayog, one of only two available then and the only one intact.

On one table in her dining room are her regular Christmas items — *gugo belens*, corn husk angels, Christmas wreaths made of *walis tingting*. From a large plastic bag on a chair she fishes out flowers which, she says, beaming, are actually made of fish scales that have been bleached, then dyed green, yellow and pink.

In another room she opens two closets whose shelves are stacked with folders and envelopes marked "Lectures" or "Materials" and sub-headed "Leaves", "Grasses" or "Seeds", and other folders containing clippings she has accumulated over the years — of articles that appealed to her because they gave additional information on local materials. From one of the closets she pulls out a folder marked "Leaves". There, on a piece of bond paper, are neatly arranged skeletonized leaves in beautiful pastel shades. The leaves can be put together to make roses which, she assures one, are really quite durable. "Mango seeds make nice flowers, too," she says as she takes some seeds out of a paper bag, "and they lend themselves very well to dyeing."

She opens a closet again, this time to take out some faded Italian-made straw hats that still carry the Aguinaldo's label. She bought the hats at the famous department store decades ago and she continues to keep them, hoping that one day she will meet someone who makes hats and would like to improve them.

"Our hats," she frowns, "look quite awful. The heads are always round, like a melon."

Like a fairy godmother, she waves her magic wand and uncovers even more marvelous treasures. Corn husk poinsettias, dyed a bright red, which will last from one Christmas to the next. The bark of the coconut, which can be turned and twisted to make balls. The flower-shaped part that closes the coconut. The coconut leaves that can be braided to make a unique divider, such as the one she has. And the lowly *tingting*. Even freak coconuts have their uses.

"So what do you need, what do you have — that is my approach. I'm not going to look in a shop because that's too expensive."

"I've never had this desire to have a chandelier, that sort of thing," she says. "When I need or want something, I think of the simplest, least expensive way."

It is the philosophy that has always guided the business that grew out of a housewife's hobby. George and Susie Winternitz had fled Austria — and Hitler — in 1938 and sought refuge in Manila, where they had relatives. The couple also hoped that Dr. Winternitz could make good use of his specialization in the treatment of tuberculosis, then the primary cause of death in the Philippines. He was never, however, able to practice medicine here, going instead into teaching and later, business.

Ms. Winternitz had loved the outdoors even as a child. She remembers having spent long hours in the woods with her parents and trips to the country with her cousins in the summer. The wealth of natural resources in her new country astounded her. The first thing she ever created out of local Philippine materials was a lamp with a *kalan* for a base and a shade of rice straw. "As time went on, people liked what we had and I made more, some for presents, until it became a business."

The business, called Georganson Manufacturing, recently moved to new quarters at the Communication Foundation for Asia, where Ms. Winternitz hopes to be able to fulfill a cherished dream. She would like to teach the nuances of her art to wider audiences, particularly in the depressed areas. Other people, she insists, can handle the manufacturing end; what would make her very happy is to see people doing what she has started by the thousands, even by the millions.

It breaks her heart that people would rather buy than make in this country where imported means best. But in Europe and the United States, where her products have found appreciative markets, she reports happily that there is emerging a return to nature.

"Young people now hardly know Philippine materials," she sighs in frustration. "I had somebody here to whom I said, How do you like my coconut leaves? And he said incredulously, Is that what it is? People don't know what abaca is, how the abaca plant looks. And what's *buri* — what part of the *buri* plant does the fiber come from? Very few people can really tell you what you need to know."

After 43 years in the Philippines, of which she is now a naturalized citizen, Ms. Winternitz still wishes she could take a boat around the country and find more things. Years ago, she recalls, her family had a boat which they used to explore beaches and coves. There is hardly time or opportunity for that sort of adventure these days, however, for Ms. Winternitz is, besides being a nature arranger, also the overseer of all SOS Children's Village activities in the country. In the '60s, she and her husband introduced the concept of SOS, which had originated in Europe. Today, there are five villages in the Philippines (in the cities of Lipa, Cebu, Tacloban, Calbayog and Davao) that provide permanent homes for orphaned and homeless children.

"My heart really is in SOS," says Ms. Winternitz.

Widowed since 1974, she lives alone in her Quezon City bungalow, an unpretentious woman who tirelessly reminds the people she meets that this is a beautiful world, this is a beautiful country.

And after this?

"Do you think," she says, laughing, "they would have driftwood and dried grass in heaven?"

Susie Winternitz retired five years ago from SOS Village, but continues to take an active interest in it. She has also eased up on her crafts making, largely because it has become difficult to transport the materials that she needs. There is no time to miss anything, she says cheerily. She spends much of her time now reading, but reports for work at her son's insurance office every day "to sign the checks."

About the Author

Lorna Kalaw-Tirol was educated at Maryknoll College and St. Theresa's College. A full-blooded Batangueña from Lipa City, she has been a journalist for almost 32 years, a wife for 28, a mother for 26. After working for years as a full-time editor at various newspapers and magazines, she has given up on Metro Manila's stressful traffic jams and opted to work amidst the quiet of her home in Antipolo. It is books she would rather do now, as well as feature articles on subjects and causes she feels strongly about.